Complete Deliverance

Complete Deliverance

Apostle Willie Tolbert

ISBN 1-58930-121-8
Library of Congress Control Number: 2004090666

Acknowledgments

I would like to take time to thank God the Father, His son Jesus Christ my Savior and Lord and the Precious Holy Spirit who inspired me with Revelation, Inspiration and Information to write this book. It has been more than five years in the making, but to God be the Glory. *It is now delivered!*

I want to thank my lovely wife, Mamie, of 29 years who has walked with me through the challenges of experiencing the lessons of Deliverance in various areas of life. Thank you for allowing me the time to complete this project. Your support always means so much to me.

I would also like to thank God for my parents, Dr. Willie Tolbert, Sr. & Missionary Ozzie Tolbert. You never considered having an abortion, but provided me the opportunity to experience my first deliverance, arriving into this world.

I want to thank the members of Yes Lord' Ministries whom I have been blessed to shepherd and have enjoyed how the Lord has taken many of you through deliverance in your own lives.

To my Apostle, Dr. Bill Smith and his wife Nadine of McKinney, Texas, who has spoken many words of wisdom into my life for which I have benefited from greatly.

Acknowledgements

To Co-Pastor Regina Gainer, an accomplished author, who took the time to read and provide a foreword for this book. Thank you for your encouragement and support.

And last but not least I want to thank Sheryl Sewell who proofed some of the early parts of the manuscript. Nicoll Stewart who spent many late nights editing and making certain the documents were transmitted to the publisher. Pastor Hector Foy, for his willingness, trust and confidence to afford his wife Cassandra the opportunity to work with me over the years. I appreciate you, Man of God.

To my EPA (Executive Pastoral Administrator) Pastor Cassandra Foy aka "C", you have worked with me selflessly for more than 8 years accepting the challenges of being misunderstood because of your loyalty, the long hours spent on conference calls, and the numerous meetings. I appreciate your willingness to serve and to fulfill your function as my EPA and Friend. Thank you for everything.

Contents

Foreword
by Regina Gainer

Society in its existence has always sought for a way of escape from its' dilemma and struggles. People would love to live a trouble free life. Life itself has its' share of circumstances, addictions and problems. The born again believer who has accepted Jesus Christ will not be exempt from trouble, but has an ability to be set free from the struggle of being overtaken by its' power. The delegated authority of Jesus Christ is that source. This authority has been given to God's people allowing them to experience victorious living. It is the exact authority that Jesus used while being here on earth confronting society's dilemma and Satan's work in all facets of life.

Demonic oppression and possession is a reality and still exists today. Its operation and activity is designed to control the believer and eventually bring destruction. Many believers have experienced freedoms in most areas of their lives, but are tormented by the recurrences of familiar struggles or spirits. Some allow the allurements of the world to bring them into bondage over and over again. The God that the believer serves is the God of power and the God of completeness. He finishes the work he has begun in the believer's life. As the believer continues to walk in Christianity, one comes to understand that "deliverance" is a process. Although deliverance is "definite," the process is not the same for all.

As you read this book written by Apostle Willie Tolbert, you will better understand the deliverance process. His experience in the ministry of deliverance has been effective in the lives of many. You will be well informed of the various and broad manifestations that can enslave the believer if allowed. You will be enlightened and educated in the authority of Jesus Christ, which has been transmitted to the believer. You will also receive knowledge and strategies that can be used to set others free from the clutches of Satan. I pray that by reading this book you will grasp and embrace all of the spiritual truths using them for your continued walk in victory. Be blessed to become a "deliverer" for others!

Regina Gainer
Christ Temple Ministries
Bloomfield, New Jersey

Foreword
by Dr. Bill Smith

In this book "Complete Deliverance" Apostle Willie Tolbert shows God's people who was in bondage and how the Lord delivered them. He clearly establishes that God through Christ has made not only the provision for our victories, but he also shows us how to work it out and live it in our own lives. I recommend this book to everyone because every one of us will find ourselves under the attack of the enemy.

Dr. Bill Smith
Christ as Life Christian Center
McKinney, Texas

Introduction

The term deliverance is used in various ways, most often in reference to an individual needing to be set free from demonic spirits. While that experience may occur, the purpose of what God has laid on my heart for this book, the message of *Complete Deliverance* goes much further. God wants to set His people free and give each of us victory over everything that would hinder us in our daily walk with Him. His desire is that we experience **total victory** in every sense of the word.

Part of the deliverance experience includes being willing to acknowledge the areas of our life where we are either challenged or have had an experience that created the need for deliverance.

This book addresses the concerns most people have such as: Why do I get to places in my life where I am being haunted by things or feelings of my past?

It is also important to identify and know that Christ has equipped each believer with the tools necessary for him or her to live victoriously. It became evident to me as a believer that I recognized the power of the Word and the Power of God. The Word of God provides several principles which I share in this book and which are vital in fulfilling the Purpose, Plan and Destiny that God has for their lives.

Complete Deliverance will benefit individuals who are determined that they must become recipients of the Manifested Word of God.

> *The Spirit of the Lord God is upon me; because the Lord hath anointed me to preach good tidings unto the meek; he hath sent me to bind up the brokenhearted, to proclaim liberty to the captives, and the opening of the prison to them that are bound;*
> Isaiah 61:1 (KJV)

> *The Spirit of the Lord is upon me, because he hath anointed me to preach the gospel to the poor; he hath sent me to heal the brokenhearted, to preach deliverance to the captives, and recovering of sight to the blind, to set at liberty them that are bruised,*
> Luke 4:18 (KJV)

To be a fulfillment of the text that is written in the books of Isaiah and Luke cannot be realized until the individual begins to walk in the ordained destiny for their life.

The Word of God expressly states that when we feel as though we are backed against a wall, stuck between a rock and a hard place, and seems as though there is no where to go; the Lord will raise a standard and move in swiftly to defend us durinig those moments of extreme pressure from temptation.

Complete Deliverance was written to strengthen the reader that no matter what challenges you are confronted with God's grace is sufficient for you. The chapters in this book are designed to walk you through your valley and bring you to a point of having a refreshing mountain top experience. You will be able to take a deep breath and go back through the valley to reclaim what the enemy has stolen. Go ahead my friend, hold your head up high, shift your shoulders straight and make your declaration. **"I have Complete Deliverance and from this day forward I will walk in Total Victory!"**

Chapter One

The God of Your Deliverance

But the Egyptians pursued after them, all the horses and chariots of Pharaoh, and his horsemen, and his army, and overtook them encamping by the sea, beside Pihahiroth, before Baalzephon.
And Moses said unto the people, Fear ye not, stand still, and see the salvation of the LORD, which he will shew to you to day: for the Egyptians whom ye have seen to day, ye shall see them again no more for ever. The LORD shall fight for you, and ye shall hold your peace.
Exodus 14:9, 13-14

When thinking about what it means to be in bondage, it is a somber thought. But many find themselves in bondage from time to time. An individual takes two steps forward, and then he's surprised to find himself several steps backward. A person thinks he is moving up, and then he suddenly hits an unseen ceiling that prevents him from progressing further. A man moves to the left and he find that he can't move any further. An individual moves to the right and suddenly it seems as if he has dropped off of a cliff.

One may wonder, will I ever get out of this dilemma? Will I ever be set free from this trap? Will oppression, suppression, repression and depression always have this stranglehold on me? Will I ever be able to lift my hands and cry, not because I'm sad, but because I'm happy? Will I ever get out of debt? Will I ever get through this sickness? Will I ever get out of this bad relationship? Will I ever be free of this predicament?

Christians love the Lord, and yet it seems that they pass from one crisis to another to another. When it looks like a glimmer of hope finally appears, suddenly a dark cloud rises and covers it. Will people ever be free? God has delivered others; can He deliver me?

Even after being healed and delivered, there are moments when it seems that there is no change. One may say, yesterday I was sure that everything was all right, but today I'm not sure. I don't know what happened between the time I laid down last night until the time I got up this morning. It looks like the sun is shining outside, but for some reason, it's so dark in here. Have you ever been there, my friend? Too many times, when these things occur, Christians decide to throw in the towel. If things don't improve to a substantial degree, then what's the use? People feel that things will just stay the way they are. They succumb to accepting being in debt as their lot in life. They begin to accept the fact that they are part of an abusive relationship. It looks like there is no hope of situations changing.

If you have been feeling any of these things, I want to say to you today, "Hold on, my friend. God has deliverance for you."

In the time of Joseph, the people of Israel had-it-made in Egypt. Joseph was so respected that the Egyptians made sure that he and his people were comfortable and well provided for. But, like many of us, the Israelites didn't realize how wonderful it was to have a roof over their heads, a meal and some change in their pockets ... until things suddenly became distorted and their environment became hostile. In former years they had been blessed and prospered; now they found themselves in bondage. Joseph had died, and new pharaohs did not remember him.

You may have experienced something similar. You are doing very well on your job, but then a new boss comes along who doesn't appreciate your past sacrifices for the company. When this happens, you may feel like God has left you. And in many of the crises of life, it seems hard to pray. This is why it is best to fast and pray regularly — before trouble comes.

Seeking God's face in the good times will prepare you for the hard times to come. The devil doesn't come after you every day, but you must be ready for him when he does come.

Now, after the event, the Israelites began crying out to God for deliverance, and God, in His mercy, heard their pleas and raised up a deliverer among them. This is one of the reasons we must take care how we treat one another. We don't know who among us will be raised up as deliverer. Moses seemed to be the most unlikely candidate, but God had permitted him to be trained in the enemy camp, and therefore he understood the strategies of the enemy.

This is one great advantage we have in the church today. Some members came out of prostitution, drug addiction, alcoholism and homosexuality. If God saved them from these things, then they have some strategic information that can be used to prevent others from falling into those vices and to help those who are already enslaved by them.

When God raised Moses up, He told him to go tell His people that he would lead them to freedom and to tell Pharaoh to let them go. Both of those tasks were challenging, but Moses believed God and set about to accomplish them.

The children of Israel represented a valuable asset to Pharaoh, and he was very reluctant to let them go. Many individuals have struggled hard to be free of drugs or some other evil because the enemy did not want them in God's camp. They were valuable to him, the individuals who were destroying homes, stealing from their employers and ruining children's lives by selling drugs to them. Satan hated to lose them. But God brought you from a mighty long way.

Moses told Pharaoh to let the people go, and ten times he agreed to do it. But each time, before they could go free, he changed his mind and refused to allow them to go. It happens today still. Someone gives his heart to Jesus, and then he goes home and turns on the television and something he sees convinces him to turn away again. Someone knocks on the door, or he bumps into someone on the street, and suddenly he is sucked back into sin.

But Moses persisted. When God is on your side, Satan cannot hold you — no matter what he tries. The people of God were not free to worship the Lord, so God said that they must go out of Egypt. Pharaoh tried to convince them that they could worship God and still remain in Egypt. That is a very old lie Satan has been telling for centuries.

The Pharaohs had placed the Israelites in bondage because they feared them. They were growing too quickly and prospering too greatly. The Egyptians feared that they would be outnumbered and overpowered. Satan hates God's people and wants to see them in bondage. He hates their prosperity and will do anything in his power to destroy it. He hates their joy and will do anything in his power to dampen it.

Pastor Mamie & I always encourage new believers, (those who have only recently come to Jesus), to be faithful in their church attendance, in Bible study and Sunday school. We encourage them to "Get in as many worship experiences as you can and spend time with individuals who are going somewhere with Jesus." All of this is necessary because Satan desires to pull them back into the world. (*Exodus 14:9*)

After the children of Israel were finally freed, the Egyptians decided to pursue after them. Sometimes the devil doesn't seem to get the message that individuals have been delivered. Oh, he's heard about it, and he's seen people doing some things they haven't done before, but he's still sure he can pull them back into his web.

When something pursues you, get focused on your goal and don't take your eyes off of it for a single moment. Just like one pursues an education, an employment opportunity or a mate, Satan pursues you.

Pharaoh's armies, with their horses and chariots, were overtaking the Israelites as they camped at the Red Sea. They hadn't captured them yet, but they had them cornered.

There is a bright spot to all of this. The enemy doesn't pursue those that he already has in his power. The fact that he is pursuing you is a sign that you are free — and you need to remain free. You broke loose from him, and that's why he is in hot pursuit of you now.

The Israelites had the Red Sea in front of them, the Egyptian army behind them, and some mountains to one side and an Egyptian fortress to the other side.

They had nowhere to go. They were trapped ... At least that's what the Pharaoh thought. What the enemy didn't take into consideration was that God was with His people. He had manifested His presence daily with them as a pillar of cloud by day and pillar of fire by night. If they remained true to Him, nothing could defeat them.

God's Word declares many things that the Israelites did not know then, nor did Pharaoh:

> *For as many as are led by the Spirit of God, they are the sons of God.*
> ROMANS 8:14

> *The steps of a good man are ordered by the Lord: and he delighteth in his way.*
> PSALM 37:23

> *I am crucified with Christ: nevertheless I live; yet not I, but Christ liveth in me: and the life which I now live in the flesh I live by the faith of the Son of God, who loved me, and gave himself for me.*
> GALATIANS 2:20

For he hath made him to be sin for us, who knew no sin; that we might be made the righteousness of God in him.
2 CORINTHIANS 5:21

I will praise thee; for I am fearfully and wonderfully made.
PSALM 139:14

Greater is he that is in you, than he that is in the world.
1 JOHN 4:4

In all these things we are more than conquerors through him that loved us.
ROMANS 8:37

Let the enemy come after you, because he can't get you unless you want to be captured. God is a deliverer, and Satan is no match for Him.

Paul stated very strongly:

For I am persuaded, that neither death, nor life, nor angels, nor principalities, nor powers, nor things present, nor things to come, nor height, nor depth, nor any other creature, shall be able to separate us from the love of God, which is in Christ Jesus our Lord.
ROMANS 8:38-39

No devil in Hell can separate believers from God's love — if they don't want to be separated. Satan cannot take an individual out of God's hand; unless he or she permits him. David knew this secret. He declared:

He that dwelleth in the secret place of the most High shall abide under the shadow of the Almighty. I will say of the Lord, He is my refuge and my fortress: my God; in him will I trust. Surely he shall deliver thee from the snare of the fowler, and from the noisome

pestilence. He shall cover thee with his feathers, and under his wings shalt thou trust: his truth shall be thy shield and buckler. Thou shalt not be afraid for the terror by night; nor for the arrow that flieth by day; nor for the pestilence that walketh in darkness; nor for the destruction that wasteth at noonday. A thousand shall fall at thy side, and ten thousand at thy right hand; but it shall not come nigh thee.
PSALM 91:1-7

So when the enemy comes after you, he will come in contact with God and be surprised. Moses said unto the people fear ye not, stand still.
EXODUS 14:13

Now, remember that they were surrounded and they had no place to go, and Moses told them not to fear.

Chapter Two

Don't Resurrect Pharaoh

The anointing within a believer is not really called upon until he is faced with something that demands it. It's not until a person is going through something, or somebody talks about him, tells lies about him, that one can know what he is made of. Truth being told, the anointing doesn't really become evident until it feels like God isn't there. It's in those moments that Christians must dig deep within the reservoirs of their souls to see what they can scrape up, and find.

When individuals come up from there, it is with an awesome praise. This is when people can magnify the name of the Lord. If His name is not exalted, He is not glorified. He is glorified when believers show that they know how to go through the storms of life, that they can bear the heartache and pains that life throws their way.

I'm talking about when no checks are arriving in the mail and the bills are due. Can you still sing? Can you still praise Him? He is glorified most, not in your good times, but in your trials and tests.

The greatest times of rejoicing recorded in the Scriptures came at the conclusion of great battles. David, for instance, wrote:

> *In my distress I cried unto the Lord, and he heard me.*
>
> PSALM 120:1

That's when believers really exalt God. Sinners see the victories and believe. Anyone can praise God when he has money. Anyone can praise God while riding in a limousine. Anyone can praise God when his stomach is full. But can a person praise Him when it seems like things are not coming together? Can people praise Him when it seems like there is a tug of war going on with their life and they're being pulled apart in the process?

When the Scriptures state that God "inhabits the praises of his people" (*Psalms 22: 3*) it means that he needs praise to enthrone Him. Many only praise God when they are quickened by the Spirit, but He is longing for something more substantial. It is time to take praise to another level. To a praise that will pierce through darkness, a praise that will not be blocked by trouble.

> *And the Egyptians pursued and went in after then to the midst of the sea, even all Pharaoh's horses, his chariots, and his horsemen. And it came to pass that in the morning watch the Lord looked unto the host of the Egyptians through the pillar of fire and of the cloud, and troubled the host of the Egyptians. And took off their chariot wheels, that they drave them heavily: so that the Egyptians said, Let us flee from the face of Israel; for the Lord fighteth for them against the Egyptians. And the Lord said unto Moses, Stretch out thine hand over the sea, that the waters may come again upon the Egyptians, upon their chariots, and upon their horsemen. And Moses stretched forth his hand over the sea, and the sea returned to his strength when the morning appeared; and the*

Egyptians fled against it; and the Lord overthrew the Egyptians in the midst of the sea. And the waters returned, and covered the chariots, and the horsemen, and all the host of Pharaoh that came into the sea after them; there remained not so much as one of them. But the children of Israel walked upon dry land in the midst of the sea; and the waters were a wall unto them on their right hand, and on their left. Thus the Lord saved Israel that day out of the hand of the Egyptians; and Israel saw the Egyptians dead upon the sea shore. And Israel saw that great work which the Lord did upon the Egyptians: and the people feared the Lord, and believed the Lord, and his servant Moses.

Exodus 14:23-31

Pharaoh's chariots and his hosts hath he cast into the sea: his chosen captains are also drowned in the Red Sea. The depths have covered them: they sank into the bottom as a stone. Thy right hand, O Lord, is become glorious in power: thy right hand, O Lord, hath dashed in pieces the enemy. And in the greatness of thine excellency, thy hast overthrown them that rose up against thee: thou sentest forth thy wrath, which consumed them as stubble.

Exodus 15:4-7

The children of Israel are in bondage in a place called Egypt. It was not so much that Egypt was a bad place, but it was the people who were bad. Earlier, when Joseph was brought into Egypt and placed into a position of prominence, (he was chosen to be the Controller, or Chief Financial Officer) over Pharaoh's treasury.

Pharaoh had a dream, and Joseph interpreted the dream. He said that there would be seven good years followed by seven lean years. Pharaoh felt that because Joseph had given the interpretation, he should suggest what to do. Joseph suggested that during the seven good years they should store up grain for the lean years. He predicted that everyone from the surrounding countries would be coming to Egypt to buy. What Joseph was predicting was not a nice thing for anybody, but God would use it to position him so that others would look up to him. When bad things happen in the lives of individuals, it is because God is positioning them to be elevated. People need to stop complaining and see what God is doing.

Complaining is a product of doubt, and it will put roadblocks in the way of God's blessings. God had been preparing Joseph for this position for many years, and it was his time to step into it, not to complain. Joseph suggested that they get a wise man to set over these matters, and Pharaoh could not imagine finding anyone wiser than Joseph.

Sometimes, when a person is employed in a place where he or she really doesn't want to work or resides in a neighborhood where that individual really doesn't want to live, it may be that God has a purpose for his or her being there.

The human, the emotional side, wants to cry out, to complain, to resist, and to rebel. But Christians need to hear what God is saying. Elijah, for example, was in the cave one day, and he was disturbed because he thought he heard God in a whirlwind. When he finally did hear God, it was in a still small voice.

Joseph proved to be a blessing to Egypt and the people there. The children of Israel had now come out of Egypt, but their tormentors were coming after them. Pharaoh, who once had them in bondage, was pursuing them. One line of speculation about why Pharaoh was so passionate in his pursuit of the children of Israel was that they had carried such riches out of Egypt with them. It's not necessary to come out of Egypt poor and with a negative attitude. It's not necessary to come out of Egypt with sickness. It's not necessary to come out of Egypt with broken relationships. People of God can come out prosperous. That's God's will for the lives of His people.

Some people have let the evils of Egypt get the best of them. Just because everyone in the family has been an alcoholic that doesn't mean that an individual has to become one too. Likewise, just because everyone around a person has been involved in drugs, doesn't mean that they have to get involved too. It's all in the attitude.

If the mind is in bondage, the whole being is in bondage. Let's say, for instance, that because an individual is male or female or disabled, he or she doesn't get any opportunities in life and that everybody is always putting him or her down. Rather than confess that, like some do, the individual should endeavor to see how they could turn their life around.

Some years ago, when I was working in a major research and development corporation, a man there said to me, "Willie, I want you to be the best at this." I was challenged by that, and I set about to learn how to operate all of the equipment. I had not gone to school to get a degree in science, but I learned so well that I later wrote a manual and made an instructional video on the operation of the machinery. When another man was chosen to work on similar equipment on the opposite side of the plant, he wasn't able to make it run efficiently as I had. I had an anointing for it, and I had the proper attitude.

When the children of Israel came out of Egypt, they were laden down with gold and silver, although they had only one set of clothes and one pair of shoes each. But, marvel of marvels, those clothes and those shoes did not wear out for the next forty years.

The children of Israel had supernatural provision, and I believe that God is setting the Body of Christ up for some supernatural provision in the days to come too. They were out and the Egyptians were pursuing them. His chief horsemen and his chariots...

Something's getting ready to appear. Something's getting ready to happen.

Understand there were those who rode on the chariots and those who rode on horses and those who were footmen. But notice what it said, "His chosen." Notice this. Look at what it says here. If a person wasn't so prosperous and valuable, why does the devil send his very best after that person?

Pharaoh (*the devil*), and his chief horsemen (*the leaders of principalities*), and the horsemen (*the demons*), pursues you. Why is it that every three to six months you repeat a cycle? Every three days you go through a headache. Everywhere you go, you stumble, and are called accident prone. Have you ever wondered? It's because you are prosperous. You got the goods. And the problem is sometimes we don't realize we have the goods.

Why do Christians run? But the Word says that they pursued them. But the rest of the text says that they went into the Red Sea.

Now the Red Sea had not been parted at this point. It was still there. And some are in a dilemma at the Red Sea. An individual can know what God has instructed him or her to do and be moving forward in what He has intended for their life, yet there seems to be a misunderstanding. One might say, "Obviously I missed something in the communication with God. I know He told me to keep my eyes straight ahead on the prize but what I see is a big deep Red Sea."

Let me explain something about the wilderness. In the wilderness one can hear everything. In Egypt you got in a comfort zone therefore you didn't hear everything because you were comfortable there. But when in the wilderness one hears the crickets. In the wilderness individuals hear all kinds of noises. I'm talking about don't resurrect Pharaoh.

The scriptures suggest, that somebody heard some noise, and speaking among themselves someone said, "Wait a minute, there's two million Jews and no one has got a horse. I hear horses. Before I hear horses. No, just sun stroke, you've been out in the sun too long. You've been out in the desert too long, you've been in this wilderness, do you need some water? No, put your ear right here." Sometimes a person can hear trouble coming. But he doesn't hear until God puts him in the place He wants the person. It was always trouble when you were in Egypt but you didn't know it, because you became immune and addicted. So, somebody, perhaps 1.9999 million persons heard and saw the horses. "They are coming!" Who's them, I thought you had the rear. I thought you were an intercessor that could hold up the church, that could hold up the pastor. Why are you trembling? They are coming. Who? Believers forget and that's why God allows people to go through some stuff because they so easily forget who is leading.

That 1.9999 millionth person was so far away from leadership he couldn't feel his help. And that's why it says no lone rangers, no man is an island. Can you understand?

So the scripture goes on that now everybody heard. And somebody said, "Moses did you forget what we said when we were in Egypt? Leave us alone." Sometimes God will lead a person to speak to someone to bring them deliverance but he is so caught up in bondage that he'll say, "Leave me alone. Leave me alone. I can figure it out." I don't know where individuals have missed this, but while in our struggle we say leave me alone. But, I'm trying to get you out. Leave me alone. But, you don't have to go through this. You deserve better. Leave me alone. But, you don't have to starve, you can eat. Leave me alone. You don't have to walk out. Leave me alone. We do deliverance at our church. Leave me alone.

So they said Moses, didn't we tell you to leave us in Egypt? Why did you bring us out here? Because there were no graves in Egypt? We were in another culture where they believed in pyramids and preserving a body.

The Egyptians have a science that is still intriguing masterminds today. They don't know how that culture could design a pyramid. So perpendicular. Not a little to the left or right, but right on point. The Jews didn't have any math of their own. But it was the Egyptians that taught them math. That's why we ought not to lag in math. I'm encouraging individuals to pursue education. I don't want to see any lazy young person this summer at home. I want to see what you're going to do, go to school and/or work.

The children of Israel repeatedly said we told Moses to leave us alone. So what, there were no graves there so you brought us out here? What are we going to do, dig our own graves Moses? It's no problem questioning God, just don't argue with Him. If he gave the answer, while you were confused you wouldn't have understood it. So the text says that God tells Moses, stretch out your hand over the sea and the Lord caused the sea to go back by a strong east wind all that night and made the sea dry land and the waters were divided. The children of Israel went into the midst of the sea upon the dry ground and the waters were a wall unto them on the right hand and on the left. But when the Egyptians pursued and went in after them in the midst of the sea, even all Pharaoh's horses, his chariots, and his horsemen. And it came to pass that in the morning the Lord looked into the host of the Egyptians, drew the pillar of fire and the cloud and troubled the host of Egypt.

Have you ever thought why did God have the pillar of cloud by day and the pillar of fire by night? It did not come until they came out of Egypt. It wasn't there while they were in Egypt, only after. See when you are bound, you can't see the leading of God because you are caught up. But God needed to put some distinction between where you were and where you are going. And so God chose a pillar of cloud by day and a pillar of fire by night and watch what happened.

When you got delivered the enemy couldn't come past the cloud or the fire. So the only way the enemy knew which way you were going was from the glory.

See when you are anointed by God everybody knows it and it is the anointing that attracts attack. But the scripture says that an angel of the Lord was before them, but when God got ready to make the transition the angel of the Lord went from before them to behind them.

Sometimes the enemy thinks he can get you because you are within eyesight, but you're not within reach. I can see something from a distance but that doesn't mean I can touch it. And so the scripture said that while the children of Israel were resting the pillar of cloud and fire was behind them but the enemy couldn't get next to them while they were resting.

As a matter of fact the enemy didn't know exactly where they were because of it. It was darkness to the Egyptians but light to the children of Israel. And they were still complaining. Remember Philippians 4: 19? But my God promised and shall supply all my needs according to his riches in glory. God is really providing for us but some of us are so blind. We can't see the provisions because we keep looking at somebody else's table instead of the Lord's table because then it says he prepares a table for me in the presence of my enemy. You've got to understand. You expect the enemy to be upset with you because he sees you've got something he can't get. He sees you putting a napkin around yourself, getting your fork, china and your silverware. Getting ready to get down on a good meal and he can't touch you.

But pastor, sometimes I sense the intensity of the enemy. It's like he's looking in on me. Well, that's possible. He's a spirit. But there's something that God put between you and him that's his protection. That's why the scripture says no weapon that is formed against me shall prosper. And if they try to get the shield down it won't work because every tongue that vies up against me in judgment shall be content for this is the inheritance because I've been left in the will.

You have got to understand, your name has been placed in the will, the testator has died and the will is activated. And so the attorney is reading off all these promises. That's why 1 Cor. 1:20 says all the promises of God are yea and amen to the glory of God our father. All of the promises, just in case you can't name them all. All of them. All the promises of God where? In Him. Are what? Yes and amen. Really I like the word yea because yea is really a word that God used back in the Old Testament to signify yea I said it. It is so. Amen.

So now the scripture moves on that the provision, that's why you can't have cursed people with you. You can't have non-tithers hanging around because they might infringe upon your blessing. It could put a freeze on your blessing. So the scripture says that the Egyptians tried to run into the provision. See, the Egyptians saw the Red Sea as the Red Sea.

But the Israelites saw it as a provision. See it all depends on how you see. So when they walked into what they known was the Red Sea carnally, spiritually it was a blessing for somebody. That's why the scripture says guard your heart with all diligence. Guard the anointing. Guard the gifts of God.

That's why you have to watch who you attach yourself to because they could cause you to have a blood clot. A blood clot is when your blood is the word coagulated. Caught. Co-agulate. That word. In other words, it gets into a lump and don't flow. And it usually gets stuck in a spot. So you have to watch who you hang with because they can clog your blood. They can clog the blood of Jesus. They can hinder you from getting your blessings.

They can set you off years. You got to watch what you eat. It could hinder you from your blessing. Listen, I see in the spirit world some of the things that God wants to do for you in the natural and I want you to be around to get it. You're not to leave everything in the will, you ought to use some of it.

Chapter Three

Understanding the Benefits of Deliverance, Part 1

What are the fruits of deliverance? Among them are joy, freedom and blessings. God has given every believer a key of authority that can use to help set other people free. Once an individual understands how to be free, he or she can then set about to use his or her newfound power to help others.

Individuals feel that they don't have to do anything. Well, just do it for the sake of doing it, because sometimes attitudes may not be right. That is something that may have to be dealt with. One can be saved, sanctified, Holy Ghost filled, fire baptized, running for Jesus all of their life and aren't tired yet and still need to be set free in an area. There are times when some of the most irritable people are anointed. What would happen if their anointed positions were taken away and their Sunday go to meeting clothes were stripped away?

Let's look at some areas anointed people are challenged with.

Bitterness –
Resentment, hatred, unforgiveness, violence, temper, anger retaliation & murder.

Insecurity –
> Inferiority, self-pity, loneliness, timidity, shyness, inadequacy, ineptness & instability.

Depression –
> Despair, despondency, discouragement, defeatism, dejection, hopelessness, suicide & death.

These are principle spirits. Under these various ones you'll find the breakout of others.

Bitterness can come with hatred, frustration and insecurity. Insecurity can come with fear, loneliness and other things of that nature. Depression always brings about rebellion.

There are two types of jealousy. One of them is good, and the other is terribly evil. There is a godly jealousy, and then there is an ungodly jealousy. The terrible type of jealousy can't stand to see others blessed. It has a space that it is always protecting.

Addictions: alcohol and drug abuse, but also addiction to food and others. Watching too much television can be an addiction. An addiction is something that has a strong influence over one's life, something that draws an individual. It's like a vacuum, sucking you in, always saying, "Give me, give me, and give me more."

Pride –
> Vanity, ego, haughtiness, importance, self-righteous & arrogance.

Strife –
> Contention, bickering, argument, quarreling, fighting, conflict, discord & turmoil.

Lust –
> of the eyes, fantasy, masturbation, homosexuality, adultery, fornication, incest & harlotry.

Control –
> Possessiveness, dominance, witchcraft & manipulation.

Passivity –
Funk, listlessness, indifference & lethargy.
Grief –
Sorrow, heartache, heartbreak, crying, sadness & isolation.
Guilt –
Shame, condemnation, unworthiness & embarrassment.
Carnality –
Control Envy, jealousy, fantasy, pride & lust.

There are seven necessary steps to deliverance. The first one is to confess your faith in Christ and in His sacrifice on your behalf.

The second one is to repent of all your rebellion and sins.

The next one is when we claim God's forgiveness of all sins.

Number four is to forgive all people who have ever harmed or wronged you.

Number five is to renounce all contact with anything of the occult or satanic.

The sixth step is to pray the prayer for release from all curses. You may say, "Pastor, I'm not cursed." Well, if poverty is in your life, that's a curse. God's people should be prosperous.

Number seven, now believe that you have received and go on into God's blessings. Those are the seven steps.

> *He that dwelleth in the secret place of the most high*
> *shall abide under the shadow of the almighty. I will*
> *say of the Lord he is my refuge and my fortress. My*
> *God and in him will I trust.*
> PSALM 91

Isn't it good to know we have safety in God?

*No weapon that is formed against me shall prosper
and every tongue that shall rise up against me shall
be condemned.*

Isaiah 54:17

The Word of God works! There are times individuals quote scriptures in his or her situation and the enemy wants to make you feel as though it's not having any effect. But it is. When you say negative things, it looks like immediately negative things start happening right away. Well, just view it on the opposite side of the track. That righteous things are happening on your behalf. Yokes are being destroyed every time you put that word out there. The enemy may be trying to come after you in one direction but when you put that word out there it's like a sword and a shield and a buckler. What does the word exclaim regarding diseases and plans coming nigh thee? He shall give His angels charge over thee. Why? To keep you in all your ways. That's why the scriptures say to delight yourselves in the Lord and He will give you the desires of your heart. In all your ways acknowledge him and he shall direct your steps. The steps of a righteous man are ordered by the Lord. They word is a lamp unto my feet and a light unto my pathway. Thy word have I hid in my heart that I may not sin against thee. The word works!

To attempt to comprehend the explanation of all the possible ways to obtain deliverance is far beyond the scope of this book. The book entitled *Blessings and Cursings*, by Derrick Prince touches on this subject. I really recommend that you all get it. Blessing or Curse you can choose.

I believe that God's people should look good. Believers shouldn't look like they just rolled out of bed. Again, balance is essential because one should not put more emphasis on the physical than on the spirit. When a believer takes care of the inside, it will reflect on the outside. Psalms 149:4 states, "He beautifies the meek with salvation." Salvation also was in the Old Testament and meaning deliverance. Remember there are three stages of deliverance or salvation here on earth.

There's the come-to-it-ness of salvation, when a person first gets saved, repents of his or her sins, confesses his or her faults, believes that the Lord Jesus died on a cross, went in the grave, rose on the third day and He is the son of God. The next stage is the is-ness of salvation. At this stage a person learns how to live saved everyday. And thirdly, is progressive salvation. Every time an individual reaches another hurdle God says that's an area that you need to grow in. You need to know how to get through this area now. Then the final and ultimate salvation is when Jesus comes back for His people in the rapture. People must be saved here in this life before they can be saved then. Simply stated, if you're not saved here you won't be saved there.

Chapter Four

Understanding the Benefits of Deliverance, Part 2

Once a person is delivered, there will be some fruit. It's like pruning a tree. Take off the dead growth and the excess foliage, and fruit comes more readily. There are some special prayers that individuals can pray that will help them to be fruitful.

Jesus spoke out very clearly about a tree that didn't bear fruit. He said:

> And now also the axe is laid unto the root of the trees: therefore every tree which bringeth not forth good fruit is hewn down, and cast into the fire.
> MATTHEW 3:10

What does it mean to be "hewn down"? It means to be cut off and forsaken.

If something is of no use and unproductive, then a person needs to get rid of it. God made us to be productive citizens. Christians must believe that they have received and go forth in His blessing.

Joseph had a great future, but to get there, he had to suffer some temporary setbacks. He was imprisoned, but because he loved the Lord, he prospered and was blessed even in the prison. His imprisonment was all part of God's plan to exalt him and bless him.

When Joseph eventually arrived at the palace of the Pharaoh, he was soon placed as second in command in the nation. This is why the enemy had fought his promotion. He doesn't want to see any of God's people promoted.

Satan sent one of his emissaries, Potiphar's wife, to tempt Joseph and lead him astray. She was assigned by Satan to abort the seed of destiny that was in Joseph.

Very early in his life, Joseph had received dreams in which he saw his brothers and even his parents bowing to him and submitting to his authority. It had not been clear to him that he would be blessing other nations.

Few of us have yet to reach our full potential in God. Few of us have yet to fulfill all of our prophetic promises. God may have given you a singing ability, or an ability in business, or some other supernatural ability, but if you have not yet seen the completion of His plan for your life, it is important not to get sidetracked. Don't let some person or some thing or some other place draw away your attention from the thing God has prepared for you.

There are many good things that you can do with your life, but there is only one right and perfect thing for you to do with your life. Believers are too easily satisfied with their circumstances and situations. God has something so much better for His people. Don't get too comfortable on a certain plateau, because God wants to move you on up higher. There's more for you.

You may think you are doing just great, and that can be a serious problem for you. You may think you are doing as well or better than others around you. You may be doing better than you were ten years ago. If you have not fulfilled God's destiny for your life, then you have more to do and further to go.

For me, it has been a wonderful thing to know that I am a spiritual father to other pastors. That's a blessing. But I dare not rest in that because I have yet not reached the height that God has determined for my life. I must continue to press forward. Until you fulfill your purpose in the plan of God, you have not done well enough in life.

Don't be satisfied to be praised by people. They will tell you how blessed they have been by your ministry. They compliment you on your good organizational abilities. That's fine, but don't be satisfied with that. That's not the ultimate goal; it's just part of the process.

You need to be delivered in your mind, in your heart and in your spirit so that you can lay hold of the excellence of Jesus Christ and glorify His name on the earth.

Be careful what you say. Many people have self-inflicted wounds. They bring curses upon themselves by what they say.

"I'm always broke."

"It looks as though everybody in my family gets sick."

"I guess I'll fail again, like before. Failure is my middle name."

Don't give voice to these fears. If you have always been broke, that doesn't mean you always have to be broke. Just because other members of your family get sick doesn't mean that you have to be sick too. Just because you have failed in the past doesn't mean that you will continue to fail. God wants to deliver you.

Claim the promises of God for your life. God said that by His stripes you are healed. He said that His highest will was for you to prosper and be in health as your soul prospers. His word declares that no weapon formed against you will prosper. He has given His angels charge over you to keep you in all your ways. He speaks that he would not put the diseases that Egypt suffered on you, that no plague would come near to your dwelling.

When God first created man, he never got sick and he never died. When God first created man, he was wealthy and prosperous. Let's get back to the garden by means of the sacrifice of Jesus, and we can have these blessings too. Everything we need is in the garden of God.

God has put in you all that you need to prosper in your garden, so if you are not prospering, you need to check your garden and see what's wrong. Is the water flowing in your garden? Is your garden being fertilized? Is your garden being cultivated? Is your garden being protected from predators?

God assigned Adam to watch over his garden. He allowed him the privilege of naming everything there. It was his, and he was responsible for it.

So check the circumstances of your garden. If there is failure, it is not God's failure. He has made the garden and given it to you to care for, but it is now under your authority. It's up to you to keep your garden well, or you may end up being put out of it.

God has planted many powerful prophetic seeds in your life. The potential in those seeds is inestimable in value, but you must care for them and see that they produce fruit. If there are not growing and producing, you need deliverance.

In Wallace Heflin, Jr.'s book, *The Power of Prophecy*, he quotes Isaiah:

> *The Lord God hath given me the tongue of the learned,*
> *that I should know how to speak a word in season to*
> *him that is weary.*
> ISAIAH 50:4

What is "a word in season"? It is the proper seed for you at that particular moment. You will not get my "word in season," and I will not receive yours. God knows just the right seed for each of us.

God never required more of Adam than he was able to do. God knew what was accessible to His servant and He knew what he could handle. He placed him in his garden and gave him power and authority to act upon.

God visited Adam in his garden:

> *And they heard the voice of the Lord God walking in*
> *the garden in the cool of the day.*
> GENESIS 3:8

And God will visit you in your garden, too.

The devil also came into Adam's garden. He had no right to be there, but he entered illegally by way of a serpent. If we allow serpents to stay in our garden, we will suffer loss. Both man and the serpent were expelled from the garden.

The twenty-eighth chapter of the book of deuteronomy outlines the blessings of God that will come upon those who obey Him and the curses that will come upon those who don't. It begins like this:

> *And it shall come to pass, if thou shalt hearken dili-*
> *gently unto the voice of the Lord thy God, to observe*
> *and to do all his commandments which I command*
> *thee this day, that the Lord thy God will set thee on*
> *high above all nations of the earth: and all these bless-*
> *ings shall come on thee, and overtake thee, if thou*
> *shalt hearken unto the voice of the Lord thy God.*
> DEUTERONOMY 28:1-2

Adam failed to follow God's laws, and he therefore, changed the course of his life. Until this time, God was welcomed in his garden, but now suddenly Adam was hiding from God. He no longer desired fellowship with his Creator, because sin had broken that bond.

Now, God didn't come to fellowship; he came to judge. He was angry because the garden had been designed as a place of longevity. It was never God's will that our prosperity be short-lived. God wanted His people to move among the elite, to belong to the special clubs and to be invited to the special parties. He wanted His people to join the Ivy League. Now that was spoiled.

Until that moment, Adam had enjoyed the fruits of deliverance, and no evil had reigned in his garden. Then, he opened the door. Evil can't rule unless you allow it. God had established a special environment in which Adam and

Eve could enjoy all of His blessings, and suddenly they had allowed an intruder to come in and damage that environment.

You are responsible to guard the ground God has entrusted to you, to work it, to watch over it, and to enjoy the fruit of it. In the end, Adam was banished from the garden prepared for him. It was a holy place, and he chose an unholy path in life. Two angels with fiery swords in their hands were placed before the garden gate to keep intruders out. No unclean thing could walk there.

"But that's my garden," Adam could have said. But no, he had given up the deed to his garden and had no more right to it. It happened when he let the devil in.

So believers must guard well what God has given to them. Keep it holy unto God and keep the Holy Ghost flowing through it. Then it will prosper. This is why we need deliverance.

Before the fall, Adam did not have to sweat as he worked in the garden. He did not need to water the ground. It was watered automatically. He never had to cut the trees down because they didn't die. And he would not have died either. He was created as a perfect man in a perfect environment.

Eden was the next thing to Heaven, and it was sometimes called Paradise.

People are still trying to find Paradise, but it's been blocked off. *Proverbs 2 & Proverbs 3:1-17*

In order to benefit from the fruits of deliverance, one must obtain wisdom.

Although Solomon's words of wisdom are directed at one addressed as "my son." They are just as convincing and powerful for daughters. My son, if thou wilt receive...

This suggests a choice. When people say that they have received something, we mean that we have acquired it, digested it, and believed it.

Many are unable to discern whether or not spiritual growth is occurring and whether or not He is manifesting Himself within their lives. Wisdom enables believers to discern it.

Most Christians discern through sight, sound and touch. This is why Scripture states:

> *Wherefore come out from among them, and be ye separate, saith the Lord, and touch not the unclean thing; and I will receive you.*
> 2 CORINTHIANS 6:17

If thou wilt receive my wisdom, hide my commandments with thee.

Adam failed in the garden because he did not hide the Word of God in his heart. He was totally submerged in the blessings of God, and yet he neglected something so important. Isn't it sad that right in the middle of enjoying God's blessings people can forget Him? Folk sometimes become so wrapped up in new houses, cars, mates and jobs and in their knowledge and money that they forget the Source of all of them. How terrible it is to concentrate on the blessings and forget the Blesser.

As children, everyone required some discipline at some point. And it doesn't matter how well a person treats his children; at some point he will forget who they are and show us disrespect or worse. Then why should people expect believers to be any different? When anyone becomes self-centered, all else is forgotten.

That's what happened to Adam. He began to focus on himself and he forgot God. If Adam hadn't been so self-absorbed, he might have recognized the danger when Eve suggested that they eat the fruit of the tree.

After we have eaten a carry-out meal, we use napkins to clean our hands and we put all the trash into a bag and throw it away. Then we feel cleansed. That's complete deliverance.

Adam's greatest failure was that he stopped walking with God. God went hunting for him, but Adam hid. He didn't want to be found.

God knew where Adam was all along. He's God. Why would He have to hunt for someone in a place where He had located them Himself? He knew, but He would not violate Adam's free will. If he didn't want to be found, God would not find him. Therefore his blessings turned into cursings.

Elijah was under a juniper tree one day, and that tree was a blessing to him. It shaded him. But when it was time for him to move on to his next assignment, God sent a worm and destroyed the tree. This is why Christians must learn to go with the flow of God's Spirit. Believers must learn to hear God's voice. You don't ever want Him to turn your blessings into curses.

When and if a blessing becomes a curse, it will not be done in secret, in some corner. Everyone will know it. At that point, there is a choice. Either a person can repent and move on, or he can be put out of the garden forever.

Verse 4, If thou seekest her as silver and searches for her as hidden treasures.

There is a vast amount of available knowledge that God wants His people to discover. It can be found by searching diligently. I've seen children put more effort into finding Easter eggs in the grass than some Christians do to find the "hidden treasures" in God.

When a person misplaces some money, he or she certainly does search diligently for it. The individual will get on his or her knees and look under furniture, dig into the dirty clothes hamper and search through the smelly clothes. What a joy it is when he or she finally finds it! But God has many "hidden treasures" just awaiting our eager search.

Then shalt thou understand righteousness and judgment and equity. Yea, every good path.

Wisdom is a great asset that everyone needs. When wisdom is acquired, many other things come with it. Wisdom will put money in your pocket. It will bring important people into your life. It will take you places you never dreamed of going.

Chapter Five

Understanding the Benefits of Deliverance, Part 3

Believers can live victoriously and without struggle. When a person enjoys the fruits of deliverance, he has a victorious life. Prior to deliverance, people are in chains of bondage and Satan can treat them like yo-yos. Why should an individual deny that they need deliverance? Why not accept the need and receive the deliverance that awaits them?

Jesus told the story of a prodigal son who fell so far that he was reduced to feeding swine. One day, he suddenly came to himself and realized that his denial of his need had crippled and bound him. There was deliverance in his father's house, and he only needed to accept it.

> *And when he came to himself, he said, How many hired servants of my father's have bread enough and to spare, and I perish with hunger! I will arise and go to my father.*
> LUKE 15:17

Why should he remain in his pitiful circumstance when there was enough and more awaiting him? He had a choice — continue to live in this impoverished way or accept deliverance and walk free, live free and have plenty. Deliverance affects everything about an individual. How he dresses, what he eats, where he goes, the things he can do.

Complete deliverance will enable you to have the anointing and the gifting you need to live a richer life and glorify God. *Galatians 5:22*

God has said that His people perish for lack of knowledge, not from too much of it, but from a lack of it. How is knowledge obtained? It is received by studying, and wisdom is applied knowledge. When speaking of the fruits of the Spirit, the Scriptures say that "against such there is no law."

Galatians 5:19-23 shows the need for order.

Fornication is sex outside of marriage. God has a law against that.

Envy is when a person sees someone else being blessed, and instead of being happy for that individual, the person is angry with him or her and tries to find something to say against that person.

Envy, strife, malice and accusations are all connected. IT involves running down somebody else's character. When one tries to destroy influence that somebody has over someone else. For example "Yeah, that's true, but you don't know what I know."

Someone else may say, "I have been so blessed by this man's ministry," and the envious person answers, "Yeah, I was too, but ..."

No one should permit himself to become someone else's garbage can. When you allow anyone to talk about another person to you, and you don't stop it, you're guilty. Rest assured that if they're talking about someone else to you, they're also talking about you to someone else.

Having the fruits of deliverance enable a believer to live right without the need for a specific law. Christians don't need anyone to tell them that it is wrong to curse. They just don't curse. Believers don't need anyone to tell them that it is wrong to be angry and let that anger remain until tomorrow. Christians don't do it. It isn't necessary for anyone to tell a believer that he should conduct hiself or herself as a lady or a gentleman before the opposite sex. Christians know to do it.

Wisdom will keep a person in the midst of any situation. It will tell the individual to walk away from a given situation and not let himself be spotted by it.

Don't argue with wisdom. When wisdom says, "You don't want to go there, to say that, to touch that," listen and obey.

When wisdom takes flight, a person is left looking like a fool. Fools don't care where they are going and if they fall into a ditch. Wisdom alerts people to the danger.

Wisdom says, "Watch out! There's a hole." Then a wise man can say, "Okay, what can I do? How can I get around that hole?"

Wisdom says, "Walk sideways, and you'll bypass the hole." Fools say, "Forget you! I'm my own person," and forge stubbornly ahead. That's why the "own person" falls into so many deep holes.

Consider this question, Are you enjoying the fruits of the Spirit, or are you still in bondage?

These verses were not written to sinners, but to the Ephesian believers. This was written to the Church. In case you haven't noticed, the Church is made up of imperfect people. The Body of Christ may be moving toward perfection, and hopefully is, but hasn't arrived yet.

When a person is saved, his spirit is saved. His spirit is born again. Jesus said:

> *Verily, verily, I say unto thee, Except a man be born of water and of the Spirit, he cannot enter into the kingdom of God. That which is born of the flesh is flesh; and that which is born of the Spirit is spirit. Marvel not that I said unto thee, Ye must be born again.*
>
> JOHN 3:5-7

People must be born again in their minds. They also must be born again in their hearts and in their spirits. Another aspect is that people must be born again in their bodies. There are people who get saved and continue exhibiting some bad habit. Jesus said further:

> *If any man will come after me, let him deny himself,*
> *and take up his cross, and follow me.*
> MATTHEW 16:24

When should this be done? Can it be done only on Sundays? Can it be done only on holidays? Clearly, individuals must take up their cross and follow Jesus daily. That doesn't mean that Christians are already perfect. As they follow Him, He strips them of the flesh and clothes believers with the Spirit. Christians have not yet arrived. Believers are only beginning. As a Christian moves toward his ultimate goal, he is perfected.

When Jesus said, "Follow Me," He said it to imperfect people. Later, before He went back to Heaven, He gave His disciples a more intimate word. It was, "Abide in Me."

When a sinner wishes to come to Jesus and be saved, he must follow Him. Then he begins to walk out of the flesh, walk out of the cares of this world, and he begins to lose his taste for this world and to move toward maturity. As he does this, he begins to get off of the baby bottle and to move on to more solid food.

When one begins to abide in Jesus, it means that that individual is no longer looking to the world for satisfaction. Now he is looking to Jesus, the Author and Finisher of his faith. As Paul knew:

> *For in Him we live, and move, and have our being.*
> ACTS 17:28

When abiding in Him, it means that a person trusts Him, and gladly follows Him wherever He chooses. He no longer struggles against God's will for his life. Individuals intuitively know that His will is best for them.

The accuser will constantly tell Christians that they cannot succeed in the Christian life and that they must look out for themselves. But as individuals grow in Christ, they come to understand the benefits of Complete Deliverance.

There is another phase of deliverance toward which everyone needs to work to reach.

> *Every branch in me that beareth not fruit he taketh away: and every branch that beareth fruit, he purgeth it, that it may bring forth more fruit.*
> JOHN 15:2

This passage is interesting because God is looking for fruit. When following Jesus, a person takes the path that He's already traveled. Christians abide in Christ must go with the flow of the Holy Ghost.

When many people are saved, they fail to accept Jesus as Lord of their lives. He can only be Lord as individuals give Him rule over their daily lives. He must be Master, and every subject is subservient to his master.

If a person is a rebel, or a hard-nosed renegade who doesn't need a leader, then that person won't acknowledge Jesus as his master. He said that every tree would be known by its fruit.

> *For every tree is known by his own fruit.*
> LUKE 6:44

God is calling each of person to be a producer of fruit. When no fruit is produced, individuals should check their connection to the vine. The enemy loves it when people try to go it alone. Many think that all they need is a little quickening from the Spirit, a shake, a dance or a jump. But that's not nearly enough. The enemy would love to get Christians hooked on feelings and make them think that feelings is all they need.

Feelings will give you a false sense of security, but abiding in Jesus will cause individuals to be fruitful in one's daily life. This doesn't only happen on Sundays; it works every other day of the week too.

Some people follow Jesus from church to church. They're in one church this week and in another one next week. They may be following Jesus, but they are not abiding in Him. When a person is abiding in Jesus, he can meet Him anywhere and everywhere, anytime and every time. When the Jesus a person knows only shows up for a few hours each Sunday morning, he is in trouble the rest of the week.

> *Now ye are clean through the word which I have spoken unto you.*
> JOHN 15:3

And how does one become clean? It is through deliverance by means of the Word of God. Deliverance brings about a purging. In our Ministry, we keep plastic bags around because sometimes all sorts of things come out of people when they are purged by the Spirit. We don't try to take people on guilt trips. We try to get them cleaned up so that they can produce more fruit.

Anytime Jesus tells believers that He wants them to produce more fruit, He is declaring their potential. If an individual was not capable of producing something more, He wouldn't bother to tell him.

What are some of the purging processes that God uses to get people ready for bearing more fruit? One way is through a word He sends that knocks on an individual's door. There is no mistaking who that word is for, and this should not be embarrassing to anyone. Thank God that He's knocking on doors. He's not there to do harm, but to make people more fruitful. He is moved by the potential He sees within His creation.

> *And he shall be like a tree planted by the rivers of water, that bringeth forth his fruit in his season; his leaf also shall not wither; and whatsoever he doeth shall prosper.*
> PSALM 1:3

When an individual's appointed season, or time, has come, there will be a purging taking place in his life so that he can produce the fruit that he was intended to bring forth. Fruit trees like apples, pears and oranges, must be vigorously pruned so that they will produce less leaves and more fruit. If not, the tree becomes less fruitful. Trees that are not pruned get top heavy and break with the wind and the other elements. Bending over is not a good sign. Things and people that are bending over need deliverance.

> *Now ye are clean through the word which I have spoken unto you*
> JOHN 15:3

If anyone doubts the power of the Word of God, that person needs help. And if any believer doesn't believe the Word, he or she needs to have someone address the portion that he doesn't believe. The reason is that when the enemy knows that a person doesn't believe, he will insist that he is right, that it simply isn't so.

Remember what happened to John the Baptist after he had boldly declared Jesus as "the lamb of God that taketh away the sins of the world"? After he was imprisoned, he sent disciples to Jesus to ask Him, "Are you he or should we look for another." He told these disciples of John to go back and tell him about the miracles they had seen Jesus do. Those believers whose faith is growing dim need to witness another revival of miracles.

People need to stop looking on from a distance and get up close where the Lord is performing His miracles. John was much too far away. He had not been in the meetings where Jesus was showing forth His mighty power.

People have turned to psychics because they have couldn't see Jesus at work in their churches. The psalmist was longing for God, until his soul fainted:

> *My soul longeth, yea, even fainteth for the courts of the Lord: my heart and my flesh crieth out for the living God.*
> PSALM 84:2

Where is He? If He is in you? show me a sign? Believers need to be able to show others what they believe, and the only way for that to happen is that they abide in Him.

Fruit is one of the ways the Lord's presence can be shown in the lives of His people. Those who don't know one tree from another will not be able to identify a fruit tree until its fruit begins to appear. So, one of the benefits of deliverance is the fruit that is produced. This makes sense, because before a person knew Jesus he was dead in his sins. Now a believer has come alive to righteousness. It has been said that anything dead needs to be buried, but in this case, anything dead needs to be pruned and purged so that it can come alive.

If there is to be a revival, it must begin in the people of God. If there is to be a river flowing, it must begin flowing through Christians. If there is to be a manifestation of God's glory, it must come through true believers having Jesus within is "the hope of glory."

According to Jesus' prayer in John 17, He has already given His Word (see verse 14), His power (see verse ??) and His glory (see verse 22) to all believers.

With the Word, the power and the glory, I would say that Christians have it made.

Blessed are the undefiled in the way, who walk in the law of the LORD. Blessed are they that keep his testimonies, and that seek him with the whole heart. They also do no iniquity: they walk in his ways. Thou hast commanded us to keep thy precepts diligently. O that my ways were directed to keep thy statutes! Then shall I not be ashamed, when I have respect unto all thy commandments. I will praise thee with uprightness of heart, when I shall have learned thy righteous judgments. I will keep thy statutes: O forsake me not utterly. Wherewithal shall a young man cleanse his way? by taking heed thereto according to thy word. With my whole heart have I sought thee: O let me not wander from thy commandments. Thy word have I hid in mine heart, that I might not sin against thee.

PSALMS 119:1-11

When it gets to verse 105, "Thy word have I hid in my heart that I might not sin against thee," it was because David had declared: "*Thy word is a lamp unto my feet and a light unto my path.*"

Jesus said, "I am the light of the world" (John 8:12; 9:5).

He said that a light is like a city on a hill. It cannot be hid. In other words, when individuals have Jesus in them, they have the Word and the light within. No one should wonder what kind of person he is. Nobody should be confused with who a Christian is.

If a light bulb starts flickering, it means either that it is burning out or that it is not well placed in the socket. As a Christian, we can only reflect Jesus if one's abiding in Him. He said, "I am the way, the truth and the light." He also said that He was the door and if any man wanted to enter, he had to come through the door. Those who came in any other way, He showed were thieves and robbers.

When a light is almost coming out of the socket it's as if it doesn't have a home. As a light abiding in Christ, (where Christians should be in Him) standing, resting and trusting in Him. All enemies have to go. They cannot remain.

When Jesus spoke saying, you have to go; He wasn't speaking to the individual. He was speaking to the spirit and saying you must go.

I see it happening. A time is coming when believers will simply speak the words! "Got to go, got to go. I'm not waiting. Go."

Demonic spirits are going to come inside the church and try to do what they normally do and (zap, zap), demons will flee. I'm believing God that the day is coming. God is teaching His people now. The day is going to come when the anointing will be so strong in the lives of believers that whenever demons come around they are going to have to either keep silent or be unable to enter.

People are going to get free at the door. Individuals are going to go under the power of God and nobody is going to lay hands on them but the Holy Ghost.

The worship team will be ministering and spirits will be evicted. That's why it's important that the worship team be Holy. During worship demons will have to go. People are going to be healed and set free. Regardless of the addiction that controls them. These spirits will have to go! Even if a demon tries to manifest, it's going to go. Children will be casting out demons, pointing their hands saying, "I see you." The evil spirits will be trembling.

Folks will be trembling at the power of God. That's how it was when Jesus got out of the boat into the Galilean country. Jesus put his foot on the ground and changed the atmosphere. Rulers and principalities said, "Oh, my throat is shaking." Remember the scripture when Jesus was on the cross? There was a trembling going on in the spirit realm. The changing of the guards.

Chapter Six

Mental and Emotional Slavery

Therefore they [the Egyptians] did set over them [the children of Israel] taskmasters to afflict them with their burdens. And they built for Pharaoh treasure cities, Pithom and Raamses.
And they made their lives bitter with hard bondage, in mortar, and in brick, and in all manner of service in the field: all their service, wherein they made them serve, was with rigor.
And it came to pass in process of time, that the king of Egypt died: and the children of Israel sighed by reason of the bondage, and they cried, and their cry came up unto God by reason of the bondage.
EXODUS 1:11, 14 AND 2:23

Under Pharaoh's authority the lives of the Israelites became bitter and without reward. Every effort toward self-improvement or freedom brought an even greater weight of servitude upon the Hebrews. This continued until their bondage became more than a lash in the hand of an angry and hateful overseer. Their utter helplessness began to bite into their very souls taking hold of their minds and spirits. In time, they became slaves in more ways than just the physical. Mental slavery is always worse than physical slavery.

This is the area where so many Christians struggle. The circumstances of their pasts have forged within them an attitude that is not easily cast aside. Even when they finally become free physically, they are not enjoying their freedom. They are still bound — in their minds.

This explains why so many people, even after receiving medical treatment and consequently having been diagnosed as healthy, tend to question whether or not they have actually experienced the healing.

To them, every tiny symptom warns of a reoccurrence of the dreaded disease. This is because so many ailments, both physical and spiritual, are the result of things people have suffered from the past — hurts and disappointments of every type. These experiences attach themselves in the minds until people are enslaved in the worst possible way.

What happened to the Israelites? They had been under an abuse of control. This had resulted in emotional control and spiritual manipulation. They had also been in financial bondage. They were being used, and they had no hope of ever regaining control over their own lives. They became victims in the worst sense of the word, which led them to become controllers themselves.

Take a look at each of these insidious evils and try to discover why the children of Israel were so anxious to be free of their oppressors yet so hesitant to leave them once their physical deliverance finally did come.

Chapter Seven

An Emotional Manipulation

The principle technique used by an abusive controller is known as emotional manipulation. It might include such things as: tears and helplessness, anger, threats and a silent treatment. These are all primary instruments of emotional manipulation. Silence, a form of rejection, is an especially powerful and emotional tool.

Many people don't need the help of others to control them. They are controlled by their own emotions, and they make all their decisions based on their immediate feelings. This is why they make such bad decisions. The biblical way of making decisions in life is to depend on the Holy Spirit:

> When he, the Spirit of truth, is come, he will guide
> you into all truth.
> JOHN 16:13

No one has a right to influence others with emotional manipulation, and certainly no one wants to be influenced in this way by anyone else.

One example of how this works would be the following: Parents sometimes resent the fact that their married children have made separate plans for holidays. One of them may begin to cry and say that the child doesn't know just how long mother or father will be around. Who knows, this might be the very last time they will all be together as a family.

This type of conduct is designed to lay "a guilt trip" on the children, and when it happens, one must begin to pray and ask the Lord for direction. This is no way to make important decisions in life.

Before responding to anyone who does this, an individual must ask the Lord to season his or her words and prepare the hearts of the manipulators so that they are not unnecessarily hurt by the rejection of their suggestions. Believers must be sound in the Word of God, and walking in the Spirit, so that they will not fall prey to emotional manipulation.

Can this type of control be compared to what the Israelites suffered in Egypt? Well, not all abusive controllers rule with an iron hand, as the Egyptians did. Some are clothed in sweetness and gentleness. But this type of controller is also very dangerous. If such a person can manifest a tear or revert to helplessness, he or she will do it. The intention will be to make the victims feel an overwhelming sense of responsibility to them.

Such controllers know how to play on the strings of guilt and pity. They control through their supposed sickness, weakness and victimization.

Although sometimes their ailments or infirmities are legitimate. More often they are fabricated or, at the very least, exaggerated. People who act like this make their victims feel that if they are not immediately pampered and petted, their whole world will fall apart.

If someone tries to make you feel obligated to change your long-established plans just to suit his or her selfish desires, say to that person, "My feelings for you have nothing to do with the circumstances. I'm sorry that you are upset, but this is just the way things are."

One must not fall into the trap of emotional manipulation by thinking that something is wrong with them. Sometimes this may call individuals to be blunt and take a stand. Agreeing with the other person is to allow oneself to be manipulated by his or hers attitude.

One wonderful guard against this evil is not to be overly dependent on other people. For instance, believers should not always expect others to pray on their behalf and get answers from Heaven. Christians must hear from God for themselves and then mature their understanding of His will through the godly counsel of faithful and proven leaders.

God has a plan for each individual, and one must not allow others to spoil it. The Lord may indeed cause a believer to understand His plan through others, but He will not lead through others. Fear will cause people to depend on other people, but the Holy Spirit wants to lead and guide personally.

Chapter Eight

Spiritual Manipulation

Spiritual manipulation is another dangerous area of control that is often exercised over others. This, in fact, may be the most dangerous of them all.

Like emotional manipulation, spiritual manipulation appeals to the soulish realm. It has nothing to do with the true spiritual realm. Those who are spiritual manipulators have not developed godly character in some particular area of their lives. They are led by their lusts and their insatiable desire to control, rather than by the Spirit of God. This is why spiritual novices face grave danger. Paul wrote to Timothy:

> *A bishop then must be blameless, the husband of one wife, vigilant, sober, of good behaviour, given to hospitality, apt to teach.*
> *Moreover he must have a good report of them which are without; lest he fall into reproach and the snare of the devil.*
> 1 TIMOTHY 3:2,7

The Apostle Paul knew the danger of promoting too quickly those who are not yet spiritually mature. Such inexperienced leaders often fall prey to the temptation of pride and tend to get puffed up when they are given some position in the church.

This same danger exists for those upon whom God has bestowed some special anointing or gift. If they have not fully matured, they often begin to feel that they are among the elite, and they consequently carry an air of superiority. They often start to look down on others whom they consider less spiritual than they are, and they even begin to abuse those under their authority, rather than loving and caring for them as they are called to do.

Our Lord has no superstars in His Church; He only has servants. If any servant does his job well, then God will promote him. No matter how great a person's name may become, if he is a true servant, he will maintain a desire to meet the needs of those in his charge and to help them when they are in trouble.

Every true servant of God must be careful not to use his God-given authority to lord it over others. In nearly every church, there are those who think that everyone should obey them because they have been there the longest or because they appear to be the most spiritual. Such people will seek to dominate every decision that is made, and they will freely offer their advice in every personal circumstance of the other members.

Believers in Christ are not to base decisions in life on the opinions of other people, especially if God has not ordained that person for leadership. Every decision should be based on the Word of God.

Paul wrote to the Romans:

> *For as many as are led by the Spirit of God, they are the sons of God. For ye have not received the spirit of bondage again to fear; but ye have received the Spirit*

> *of adoption, whereby we cry Abba Father. The Spirit*
> *itself beareth witness with our spirit, that we are the*
> *children of God.*
> ROMANS 8:14-16

Too many super-spiritual people are looking for those over whom they can exercise control. This is spiritual manipulation. When a person has a spiritual call on his or her life, these people recognize it and single that person out for THEIR special ministry. Many times such super-spiritual people are unseasoned themselves, yet they will give words that they say are from the Lord. Often this results in developing people being pushed out ahead of God's perfect timing. Liardon stated:

> *"Many genuine calls upon people's lives have been aborted because of super spiritual abusive controllers."*

How is this done? There are several ways. One way is organizing a Bible study with someone other than your pastor as leader just because you don't think the pastor is teaching what you consider to be "the deep things of the Spirit." Such Bible studies are dangerous and often lead to a church split. Believers must not fall prey to this type of spiritual delusion.

Another way abusive controllers can abort calls is by giving out false "words" from the Lord or false visions. Usually such words or visions are either extremely morbid or extremely favorable. They are designed for the same purpose: to push the hearer out ahead of God's timing and ultimately to abort the call of God upon his or her life. The truth is that the people who give out such "words" have not had a visitation from God.

The Word of God speaks strongly against those who give out false prophecies and visions. They are known simply as "false prophets," and their judgment is sure. God stated that the words spoken by false prophets against His people Israel would come back upon the false prophets themselves.

God's people should not be guilty of receiving false words that come forth from insincere people. The devil wants to destroy the calling of God and thwart His purpose in the earth. He will do it any way he can, and if one is weak in an area, this is exactly where he will attack. He will come from the direction you least expect, and unless a believer is sensitive to the Spirit, he may succeed.

Abusive controllers act as if they are spiritual people, but, in reality, their control is from the devil. He uses them to get at a believer and destroy their destiny.

Praying controlling prayers is another form of spiritual manipulation. A prayer is composed of words with a spiritual force behind them, but they are spoken, not to God, but to influence the course of someone's life. A person listens to the prayer prayed and may be swayed by it. Prayers should always be guided by the Word and the Spirit, not by any other personal desire.

An abusive controller prays his own human desires or will for someone else out of his own heart. He or she is trying to make another individual obey those selfish desires, rather than the Lord's will for that particular life. This should not be.

Well, briefly stated, those are the problems. Now, what can be done about them? It's time to find Complete Deliverance through our Lord Jesus Christ.

Chapter Nine

Now You See It, Now You Don't

It is imperative that believers become confident in the power of an almighty God and that they stand tall in His promises. This is an important and necessary element for maintaining Complete Deliverance.

The children of Israel had to receive their redemption, but that could not come until they had first identified and dealt with the source of their bondage. Complete Deliverance will never be realized unless and until a person identifies and confronts the areas of need in his or her life.

Jesus assures all believers that He has given us power and authority over every enemy. He said:

> *Behold, I give unto you power to tread on serpents and scorpions, and over all the power of the enemy: and nothing shall by any means hurt you.*
> LUKE 10:19

*He has also made us to know that the devil is already
defeated. Now is the judgment of this world: now shall
the prince of this world be cast out.*
JOHN 12:31

*And having spoiled principalities and powers, he
made a show of them openly, triumphing over them
in it.*
COLOSSIANS 2:15

If Jesus had not overcome Satan, everyone would be in
trouble. It would be impossible to resist him if Jesus had not
first put him in his place. Now believers can do that:

*Submit yourselves therefore to God. Resist the devil,
and he will flee from you.*
JAMES 4:7

Christians can resist him by putting on "the whole armour
of God":

*Put on the whole armour of God, that ye may be able
to stand against the wiles of the devil.*
EPHESIANS 6:11

*Wherefore take unto you the whole armour of God,
that ye may be able to withstand in the evil day, and
having done all, to stand.*
EPHESIANS 6:13

*Above all, taking the shield of faith, wherewith ye
shall be able to quench all the fiery darts of the
wicked.*
EPHESIANS 6:16

In writing to the Romans, Paul showed that God's people
can be victorious in all things. After naming many difficult
trials, he declared:

Nay, in all these things we are more than conquerors
through him that loved us.
ROMANS 8:37

For sure, there is nothing to sing about in this world except heartache, pain and loss. But believers have many reasons to rejoice. God offers redemption. Those who are in bondage have no song, but for the people who God moves mountains and leads across seas, they can sing.

For four hundred years (commonly referred to as the silent years) between the voice of the last prophet Malachi and the coming of Christ, there was no song. Then, suddenly, the heavens were opened and both angels and men sang for joy. The Scriptures contain examples of songs. There is the "Magnificat" of Mary (see Luke 1:46-55), the heavenly chorus in the shepherd's field (see Luke 2:13-14) and the rejoicing of Simeon and Anna in the Temple in Jerusalem when they saw God's redemption (see Luke 2:25-39).

The victory chant of Exodus 15:21 expanded into a thanksgiving psalm. Its starting point was the destruction of Pharaoh's army, but it went on to develop the theme of God's power and His care for His people: the wonders of the exodus, the conquest of Canaan, even the building of the Temple in Jerusalem. The Lord has proven to be our Deliverer, Protector, Sustainer, Provider, Saviour, and Guide, our God! Thank you Jesus!

One of the unique facts regarding Israel's Deliverance was that when the people cried out because they saw Pharaoh, the Lord said *"Why cry out to me, use what you have in your hand"* (the staff). (Exodus 14:26)

Now when one has COMPLETE DELIVERANCE, there is manifested evidence that assures that Deliverance is complete.

In order to achieve Complete Deliverance, it is imperative to trust the Lord every step of the way and follow His instructions. The major reason why some people find themselves repeating old habits, is because they look back and try to associate themselves with the people, places and things of the past.

The Apostle Paul states:

> *Brethren, I count not myself to have apprehended, but this one thing I do, forgetting those things which are before. I press toward the mark for the prize of the High Calling of God in Christ Jesus.*
> PHILIPPIANS 3:13-14

Chapter Ten

The Power of Forgiveness

For thou, Lord, art good, and ready to forgive; and plenteous in mercy unto all them that call upon thee. Psalm 86:5

And forgive us our debts, as we forgive our debtors.
MATTHEW 6:12

But that ye may know that the Son of man hath power on earth to forgive sins, (he saith to the sick of the palsy,) I say unto thee, Arise, and take up thy bed, and go thy way into thine house. And immediately he arose, took up the bed, and went forth before them all; insomuch that they were all amazed, and glorified God, saying, We never saw it on this fashion.
MARK 2:10-12

There is great power in forgiveness, and many have not yet discovered it. It would be so sad for anyone to go to his or her grave carrying something unnecessary.

Then said Jesus, Father, forgive them; for they know not what they do.
LUKE 23:34

Far too many Christians find it hard to forgive the offenses committed against them in the past. Sometimes, fifteen years later or even longer, they still remember and harbor things in their hearts. They constantly remind the other person of what he or she did to them. But whether it was yesterday, a year ago or ten years ago, Christians must learn to forgive in order to have God's blessings upon their lives.

Unforgiveness is one of the greatest hindrances to receiving an answer to prayers, and it will stop the flow of the power of God as quick as anything else.

Oftentimes believers seem to be rising in their Christian experiences, only to hit a snag and actually begin to slide back down. It seems that they hit a bump in the road, and suddenly can't go any further. Certain challenges or trials seem to stall progress and prevent believers from moving forward. If the truth were to be known, many times these problems could be traced back to some unforgiveness on their part.

As Dennis Rainy wrote in his book *Staying Close*, forgiveness is freeing. Some sicknesses are due either to a lack of forgiveness toward others or the failure to seek forgiveness from others who have been offended by them. Thank God that He is forgiving, and He calls believers to be forgiving, too.

Everyone is imperfect and therefore needs forgiveness. Everyone will, at some point, be offended by others and will need to be forgiving toward them. How terrible it would be to go to the grave carrying unforgiveness. When God has been so merciful, how can one be any less merciful with others?

Many times offenses are due to nothing more than misunderstandings, but whether that is the case or not, it's not worth getting old before time to harbor unforgiveness toward another person. What some other person did or didn't do is not worth losing sleep over.

Some people seem to have a gift of offending others, and they may not be intelligent enough to know the importance of seeking forgiveness. But this type of irresponsible conduct cannot be allowed to stop the people of God from enjoying God's blessings upon in life.

The Lord is "good" and He is "ready to forgive." Those two truths go together. When a person is "good," he or she will also be "ready to forgive." How can an individual not forgive, since God has forgiven them?

When a person doesn't think that they have ever done anything wrong, they need to be enlightened. Everyone does wrong. Still, God has not thrown anyone out of His house. He hasn't turned His back on the world. He still loves people — as "messed up" as they are sometimes. He is "good," and that means that He is also "ready to forgive." He is "plenteous in mercy unto all who call on Him."

This should not be news to anyone. After all, Jesus is our Advocate, and He sits on the right hand of the Father making intercession for believers. Why would a person need anyone to intercede for him or her? Because everyone "blows it" sometimes. People "mess up." In plain words, sin. And it doesn't matter how saved or sanctified a person is. It matters not how much Holy Ghost resides within a person. It doesn't matter how many times one has spoken in tongues, prophesied or laid hands on the sick. There comes a time in life when every person needs God's forgiveness.

There are sins of commission, or wrongs that are committed, and there are also sins of omission. These sins are things that should have been done and weren't, areas where people have missed the mark of God's best for their lives. Usually, when a person has committed a sin, he or she knows it, but sins of omission are often unknown to him or her.

The intercession the Lord Jesus performs at the right hand of the Father is not for sinners, commonly called unbelievers, but for those who love Jesus and have accepted Him as Lord and Savior. Christians need His intercession. They are far from perfect, and do wrong things.

If God had not been willing to forgive, where would any of us be? If He had not shown mercy over and over again, how could people exist? Everyone ought to thank God for His forgiving spirit that frees from a sure doom and gives eternal life.

When a person asks God for His forgiveness, it is not because he or she deserves it. Just the opposite is true. But when asking for His forgiveness, it is because He is "good" and because He is "ready to forgive."

When individuals sin, and seek God's forgiveness, they make many promises to Him, that they will never do it again, that they've learned the lesson once and for all or that they are deeply sorry for the wrong they have committed. Tears even accompany their words. All too often, the same offenses are repeated, but still the Lord is gracious to forgive.

David knew what it was to need God's forgiveness:

> *Look upon mine affliction and my pain; and forgive*
> *all my sins.*
> PSALM 25:18

God is more than ready to forgive. Even before a person thinks of sinning against Him. He has prepared a way for him or her to be forgiven. I'm not talking about playing God for a fool. I'm not talking about mocking God, seeking His forgiveness and then purposefully going back to the vomit over and over again. If a person keeps that up, there is no forgiveness and he or she just might die in his or her sins. Never take God for granted. But if an individual loves Him and needs His forgiveness, He is "ready to forgive", even now.

As part of His teaching to the disciples on prayer, Jesus spoke these words:

> *And forgive us our debts, as we forgive our debtors.*
> MATTHEW 6:12

So God has tied His willingness to forgive to a person's willingness to forgive others: *"forgive us ... AS we forgive."* That must be a scary thought for some, because they are not forgiving. This word debt helps to understand something about forgiveness. A wrong is a debt, and when an individual asks God for forgiveness, he or she is asking Him to wipe out his or her debt, to cancel it, to eradicate it, to get rid of it. That's all well and good, but a person must be willing to do the same. People want the mercy of God for themselves, but they are unwilling to extend His mercy to others.

Jesus told the story of a man who had been forgiven a very large sum of money by his creditors. Rather than be thankful and show mercy to others, he went that same day and found a man who owed him a measly sum of money. And when he did, he treated that man very harshly, threatening to imprison him if he didn't pay up.

When word of this terrible injustice reached the ears of the man who had forgiven the first so much, he was understandably outraged and bent on revenge. Jesus said that a man who would be so ungrateful and unforgiving would be cast into outer darkness.

When God forgives, He gives grace to forgive others. If individuals are unwilling to extend His grace to another person, woe unto them.

Jesus has *"power to forgive sins"* (Matthew 9:6), and Christians need that power. A person could live what seems to him or her a "sinless" life and still fall short of God's glory.

Every individual has faults in his or her life, but God doesn't cast people out because of it. He lets a person know that there are areas that he or she needs to work on, areas where the person needs more maturity. These faults can be corrected and avoided in the future.

There are several levels of the salvation experience. In the first level, "I am a sinner and I ask God to cleanse me of all sin." God's loving response to individuals is to put it all behind them. It's suddenly gone, and they are clean. How could anyone do less for a person who has offended?

In the second level of salvation, ——when there is something often called a progressive sanctification, "I'm already saved from past sins, but I notice that I'm not perfect in my daily life and that I need more than forgiveness from past sin. I need the Lord's forgiveness on a daily basis. My attitude is not always what it should be. My words are not always what they should be. My actions sometimes fall short of my spiritual desire. I need to learn to walk in the light of Jesus."

> *But if we walk in the light, as He is in the light, we have fellowship one with another, and the blood of Jesus Christ his Son cleanseth us from all sin.*
> 1 JOHN 1:7

What does His blood cleanse a person from? It cleanses individuals from all sin, and this promise is for those who "walk in the light." Everyone needs God's forgiveness, and all must extend His forgiveness to others. A Christian must not be so hard on himself and also must not be so hard on others.

If God hadn't made being a Christian easy, many would not qualify.

No one could afford the cost. And if He expected immediate perfection most if not all would fail. If a small child were offered keys to a car and told to drive it, the child might be fascinated by shiny keys, but he or she certainly could not drive the car. In the same way, God knows what level of spiritual development a person is in and He won't expect something from that individual that he or she is incapable of fulfilling.

It takes time to reach maturity, and no one knows that better than God. He gives time to reach the next level, and He doesn't condemn for not becoming full adults immediately. Later, when looking back and examining the before person and the now person, any individual is amazed. If a Christian has been walking with Jesus longer than another person, he or she shouldn't be so harsh on them. That person will grow, just like the more seasoned Christian has grown.

Jesus was about to heal the man who was sick with palsy, but first He forgave his sins. Many times, when people request prayer for healing, the best thing to do is to pray with them for the forgiveness of sins. In most cases, if their sin can be forgiven, they will be healed. Not everyone seeking prayer for healing has sin in his life, but many do. And others have unforgiveness. Forgiving and being forgiven are powerful healing tools. When this man had the palsy, the people did not realize that Jesus had the power to forgive. He said "My friends, Jesus is willing to do the same for you today. You may ask the question how can a man who I do not know personally would be so kind as to forgive me of my sins?" Well, Christians must tell their neighbors the good news that Jesus died on the cross just for people who are in the same situations that didn't know. I really could conclude the sermon right there. Because many times humans complicate God. They complicate what church is all about. People make Christianity seem difficult. Christianity is really an alternative lifestyle. You'll be blessed real good by this truth. Here's a genuine definition for an alternative lifestyle. When a person gets tired of being sick and tired of being sick and tired, he or she can come be a Christian. If an individual gets tired of his or her body being abused, misused and false accused, I have an alternative, become a Christian. If a man or woman, boy or girl is tired of feeling like he or she is down and out, no one cares, that is the best time to become a Christian.

Well, Pastor, Pastor, I want to take you up on your offer but I need you to answer this one question. If I decide to become a Christian will I have any more troubles? Will I have any more problems? Will I ever get sick again? Will my money ever get funny? Will people ever talk about me?

Will the sun always shine? Do you know the answers to these questions? Yes. You may wonder, "Pastor, what is the distinct difference? What is the difference between now and then?"

Well, right now, you are by yourself. When you're a Christian, you're with Christ. Christ says, "Whatever you get in your life, cast all your cares upon Me. Why? Because I care for you." As a matter of fact, it's in your benefit package, the bible. The B in the Bible means benefits. Didn't you know that? There are many Christians living beneath their privileges outlined in the word of God. Most people don't know that they can walk in divine health? Look it up in the benefit package. Individuals can walk in divine wealth. Again, this can be found in the benefit package. The scripture says that benefits don't only come on Sundays, but it is recorded in Psalms he daily loadeth us with benefits. Some people may work on jobs or are involved in places of employment that may not offer benefits because of part time status. So maybe if individuals stop being part time Christians, they'll get benefits. What are part time hours? Part time hours are anything less than full time.

I've got a lot of folks nervous now, but I need to interject this here. When Jesus was hanging on the cross, he was not just hanging he was nailed to the cross. Can you visualize nails going in your hands? Can you feel the pain? While he was hanging there if anybody had any rights to say the hell with everyone it was Jesus. I think I've got your attention]. But He said, "Father, to heaven I speak. Forgive them of their sins for they know not what they do." I know that some people would find it extremely difficult to find in their sane mind, and sound mind how could it be that somebody who's every-day habitually doing the same harassment, the same antagonism to individuals every day, how is it that they don't know what they're doing? [Oh listen, I feel the holy ghost right now]. Jesus said it's deep within the deep. He said they may perform some actions but they don't know the value of the person to whom they are applying the action. Many people don't realize that as a child of God, you are highly favored of the Lord and the more strikes they put on you, the more they pierce you in your side, the more they mess with your mind, the more they mess with your money, the greater victory you'll have! The more you endure God is going to bring you out for the Scriptures declare, *"Many are the afflictions of the righteous but the Lord delivers them out of them all."* When the enemy comes in like a flood wanting to submerge you in your dilemma, wanting to drown you in your situation, the spirit of the Lord will lift up and stand and say that's enough. God said, "I won't put any more on you, than you can bear." Remember, whatever you're going through, God gave you the grace to go through it. And if God doesn't put more on us than we can bear, God is saying why would you put more on yourself than you can bear. While hanging on the cross, Jesus said, "Father, forgive them." He could have called 10,000 angels and wiped every single Roman soldier out.

He could have called angels and said, "Now go to the houses of those that said crucify me. But no, he said, "I'll defeat the purpose by doing this. I will forgive." As the author and the finisher of our faith, Jesus wanted to show believers how to handle situations.

Everyone has experienced someone doing them wrong. And vice versa, everyone has wronged someone. But guess what, Jesus forgave and still forgives us. Even sins we will do tomorrow. Whoa, you may ask, "Am I going to sin tomorrow? Well, you don't have to. What you do affects others, but Jesus says, "Father, forgive." Jesus did this in a difficult situation, in his adverse state while being crucified. How many

Christians could do that? Forgive them, Lord. Most would say, "No, I'm going to pay them back. Just watch. I'm going to get you." And that's why the Solomon wrote, "hell has no fury like a woman's scorn." That's deep. Jesus in the midst of his dilemma said, "Forgive." Now people must understand that they may be in a crucified situation, seamlessly like there isn't any help or hope. But God's grace says, "Forgive." When Stephen was being stoned, the bible says, he looked up, just like Jesus. Believers must begin to look up and say, "Father, forgive them." But notice, there are times when we might be the ones who are sinning. Jesus, looked up, he didn't look down. If he would have looked down, He might have said, "I want 50 million angels to come down and wipe them all out." But he didn't. He looked to where His help came from. He couldn't look at it because every time he looked at it, he felt the pain even more.

But pastor, I wasn't there. I didn't hang Jesus on the cross. I didn't pierce him in the side. I'm innocent. Are you really? Every time we go against the perfect will of God we're putting Jesus back on the cross. We're telling the devil, "You did a good job!" How many individuals are grateful that Jesus forgave? We all should bless Him with our whole hearts.

We normally ask everyone to bow their heads and close their eyes when we pray, but everyone was looking at Jesus when he prayed. Through His actions He said, "I'm not ashamed. If you weren't ashamed to beat me, if you weren't ashamed to pierce me in my side, if you weren't ashamed to put a crown of thorns on my head." Have you ever felt the effect of a nail whether you accidentally rubbed up against it, or stepped on it? It's a pain that stings so much that you think the nail is still in there, but it's gone. Don't let any sweat or salt get in the wound that only compounds the pain. This is what happened to Jesus for you and for me. With His hands up, He couldn't even wipe His sweat. The bible states that His sweat came down like drops of blood for you and for me.

Jesus said, "I thirst." The people didn't understand Him. They didn't give Him ice tea, cool water, or soda. They gave him feneca-gall. This means they added something to His suffering. Are you thirsty? They didn't even put it in a cup, but a sponge. Sponges carry fragrance. It carried the odor of the vinegar and the gall. Did anyone say, "Enough is enough, take him off the cross. I'm going to give my life for Him?" No, Jesus hung up there for you. He would not come down from the cross just to save Himself but He stayed there for you and for me. After reading this book anyone challenged to say, "Yes, I want Jesus in my heart. I don't want to be guilty of putting Him on the cross." Will you say yes to the Lord? If you don't know Jesus as your personal savior won't you say yes I want to give my heart to Jesus? Pray this prayer now;

Lord Jesus, I repent of my sins. I ask You to forgive me of every sin that I've committed against You. I believe that You are the Son of God and that You died and rose again giving me victory over sin and Satan. Lord, I accept You into my heart as my personal Lord and Saviour. Thank you for shedding Your blood for me an accepting me into Your family. I thank You and bless Your wonderful name. I exalt You, for You alone are worthy of praise.

In Jesus name, Amen!

Thank God for another soul being won to His Kingdom! Heaven rejoices with you and welcomes you to the family of God! Alleluia!

Chapter Eleven

This is the Day of Deliverance

Then David said to the Philistine, "You come to me with a sword, with a spear, and with a javelin. But I come to you in the name of the Lord of hosts, the God of the armies of Israel, whom you have defiled. This day the Lord will deliver you into my hand, and I will strike you and take your head from you. And this day I will give the carcasses of the camp of the Philistines to the birds of the air and the wild beasts of the earth, that all the earth may know that there is a God in Israel. Then all this assembly shall know that the Lord does not save with sword and spear; for the battle is the Lord's, and He will give you into our hands.

1 SAMUEL 17:45-47

Thus says the Lord to you: Do not be afraid nor dismayed because of this great multitude, for the battle is not yours, but God's.

2 CHRONICLES 20:15

This is the day of deliverance from every giant that has been oppressing God's people. God chose an anointed vessel by the name of David. He was not an army man, but the army men were cowering in fear, having succumbed to the negative influences of the intimidation, fear and doubt. This was startling because they represented God and His people. In the past, every time they had gone out to fight, God had gone before them and given them a supernatural anointing to fight and defeat any enemy. They were very human, but with God on their side, they were always victorious. But something had happened to them. A giant of a man, one of the Philistines, was daily threatening them, until they had lost all hope of overcoming him.

It was into this dismal setting that young David stepped. He was shocked by what he saw and asked his fellow Israelites what was going on. Why was an unbeliever able to overcome the people of the living God? Why were the soldiers of the Lord's host cowering like dogs behind any available protective surface? These were strong men, and they were well armed, but they were acting like children.

That reminds me of many Christians I know. They are powerful until they have to face an enemy. Then, suddenly, they are shaking in their boots. It's not wrong when believers feel that they have limitations, because they do, but it is wrong to distrust the goodness of God and His ability to rescue His people from any danger. He promised that He will never leave or forsake His children. He will be with believers till the end of the world.

I don't always understand what is happening in my life, but because God is with me, I don't worry about it. Regardless of the circumstances of life, believers can trust Him and stand on His Word. Not one jot or tittle of it will fail even until the earth passes away, and I see that the Word is still here.

Christians must not let anything separate them from the love of God. Every now and then they need to go to God's filling station and let Him fill them up again with the mix He knows is best for them. If a person has been giving out and sowing into the lives of others, there comes a time when he needs to get to the station and be refilled, refreshed and recharged. It's necessary because there are many things ahead that both will have to go through.

I would love to be able to tell people that there are no more problems, trials and tribulations once you have become a Christian, but that's just not the case. Just because an individual has accepted Jesus and become a part of His family, His enemies become the individual's enemies, and trials will increase.

But this is nothing to be worried about. "Be of good cheer," He says to all believers. "You will overcome this, and at the end of the day, there is a prize awaiting you. This is your day of deliverance."

The soldiers told David about the giant named Goliath. What was it about this man Goliath that made men fear him so much? It was the fact that he was so huge and that he was so mean and threatening. The enemy knows that believers are not afraid of tiny demons, so he sends some terrifying ones to attack anointed people, but God gives an anointing to defeat even the largest of enemies.

For some people their tormentor is physical illnesses. For others, it is problem relationships. For still others, it might be money or job status. Whatever demon that threatens to destroy life, God says that He wants to show that He can defeat the big things just as easily as He can the small things.

He was the same God who had given the Israelites victory over the Philistines again and again. This big man was no problem for Him. But, for the soldiers of Israel, this new giant was a terrifying threat. They had never one to war against him, and the thought of it filled them with dread.

What does this mean? People are accustomed to handling headaches and back pains, but when it comes to people stricken with lupus, cancer, high blood pressure or who have disfigured faces, that's all new.

The Scriptures declare:

> *Jesus Christ the same yesterday, and to day, and for ever.*
>
> HEBREWS 13:8

If God could give victory in David's day, He can do it again today. When Goliath showed up, it was not to display his lovely uniform. Pastor Mamie and I visited a museum in Philadelphia, and there we saw the uniform worn by Roman soldiers. We wondered how any man could have moved around with all of that armor on. But it was intimidating.

If Goliath was anything, he was intimidating. This man was nine and a half to ten and a half feet tall, and he had a coat of mail that weighed about a hundred and seventy pounds and a spear described "like a weaver's beam." I looked that up, and it means that it was as big as a log. It's hard to even picture it. Goliath was terrifying enough, but he also had brothers who were large, and there were other giants among the Philistine troops that day. No wonder the Israelite soldiers were frightened.

This word Nephilim is Hebrew and means "violent, or causing to fall."

These giants were violent men who fell upon others. This may be derived from a root signifying "wonder, enhanced, monstrous or proteges." (Genesis 6:4) (Numbers 13:33) A name given to a Canaanish tribe, a race of large stature, the sons of Anak. The revised version simply reads Nephilim. The Hebrew word raphilim means "a race of giants (Deuteronomy 3:11) who lived on the east of Jordan from whom Og was descended." Og was said to be so big that when someone stuck a knife in him, it disappeared and could not be seen. They thought he was sleeping, but he was already dead.

Giants have a way of blocking. We then begin to wonder if God can give victory over them. But why doubt? Look past the giant and see what God is doing. David refused to be intimidated by the giant:

*Then David said to the Philistine, Thou comest to me
with a sword and a spear and a javelin, but I come to
you in the name of the Lord of hosts, the God of the
armies of Israel whom you have defiled.*
I SAMUEL 17: 45

Notice what David did. This is an important lesson. He
knew that he could not handle this giant himself. Therefore,
he did not approach the giant in the name of David. He certainly didn't do it in the name of Tolbert. He approached the
giant only in the name of the Lord. He was David's authority.

When a ten-foot-tall man faces a small boy, there is no
comparison. Goliath mocked. You're treating me like a dog?
You're trying to play with me? You're trying to toy with me?
He said I'll make you into mincemeat.

Here's the key. As always, the enemy was looking at the
physical, but he knew nothing of the dynamics of the spiritual. He was looking at David as someone who had no doubt
failed before. The enemy looks at an individual as someone
who has frequently succumbed to sickness. He looks at people
as folk who have never been able to hold on to money. "Yet,
having the knowledge of who we are and what we are in God,
we can overcome him.

Chapter Twelve

The Grace of My Deliverance

And he said unto me, my grace is sufficient for thee. My strength is made perfect in weakness. Most gladly therefore will I rather glory in my infirmities that the power of Christ may rest upon me. Therefore I take pleasure in infirmities, in reproaches, in persecutions...

2 CORINTHIANS 12:9-10

My brethren, count it all joy when you fall into diverse temptations knowing this that the trying of your faith worketh patience. But let patience have a perfect work that you may entire, wanting nothing.

JAMES 1:2-4

It is important for Christians to understand that after being delivered from Egypt they will still experience some moments in their Christian walk where they will go through continued deliverance. Now before anyone becomes disfigured, I want you to understand I'm not necessarily referring to demons.

Usually when the term deliverance is used, immediately many people think that a person must have to be delivered from some demons. Now that may be somebody's situation, but that's not where I'm going. But what people need to understand is that when they got saved their soul got saved. The flesh has got to catch up.

Remember, there are three levels of salvation. There's the **come-to-it-ness** of salvation when individuals repent of their sins, confess their faults and believe in the Lord Jesus Christ that God has raised him from the dead and that He sits on the right hand of the Father always interceding for people.

Then there's the is-ness of salvation, where a person constantly works out his or her salvation. Because Paul said that, "When I desire to do good evil is always present." I know some people know that God has put them in heavenly places, but they are not in Heaven yet. And so understanding that as a believer goes through the **is-ness** of salvation, that individual learns day-by-day that he or she needs to rid himself of other gods. Learning day-by-day that a person has some feelings he or she needs to get rid of. Day-by-day learning that God is still working His perfect will out in a believer's life.

James Cleveland wrote a song; he said, "Please be patient with me. God is not through with me yet. But when God gets through with me, I shall come forth as pure gold."

Ultimate sanctification, the last stage of salvation, is when God will save His people permanently. When a person gets saved, he or she is saved from sin, but not from the presence of sin. God ultimately will free Christians from the presence of sin, where sin will no longer have any rights to them.

And He said unto me, my grace is sufficient for thee. My strength is made perfect in weakness. Most gladly therefore will I rather glory in my infirmities that the power of Christ may rest upon me. Therefore I

take pleasure in infirmities, in reproaches, in neces-sities in persecutions, in distresses for Christ's sake for when I am weak then I am strong.
2 CORINTHIANS 12:9-10

In the verses leading up to this passage Paul has shared his credentials, that he is an apostle. He states that God uses him and gives him great revelation, and that many signs and wonders followed his ministry.

With all of this, Paul had something that kept him in line, something that kept him in check. Everyone whether he or she speaks in tongues or not must be kept in check. God is able to do that. He does not go through the expense of saving people, only to risk losing them.

He has delivered some Christians from big things, major things, and even things that people don't want others to know about. But God did it. He dug through an entire pile of trash to find people and make them a treasure. The scripture says… in us we have this hidden treasure in earthen vessels. He saw value in His creation.

There are three reasons that God refused to remove the thorn from Paul's flesh. This man had such a deep relation-ship with God that he spoke prophetically. He had the gift of the word of knowledge and the gift of the word of wisdom. In fact, all of the gifts of the Holy Spirit were in operation in his life. He was in close contact with God, and yet there was something bothering him. He didn't understand the thorn he was experiencing in his flesh.

Maybe the Lord had forgotten it. After all God was very busy healing sick people and delivering those who were op-pressed. So Paul prayed fervently, not just once, but three times, that this thing would be removed from him.

The answer he got each time was the same: *"My grace is sufficient for you."*

Paul must have been sure that he could do a greater work if this thing (whatever it was, the Bible does not say) was removed. He thought that he could go to higher heights and deeper depths and allow nothing to separate him from the love of God if God would only hear this prayer. He would speak to mountains and they would be removed if the Lord would help him.

Why the Bible is silent about what bothered Paul so much, we cannot say. Apparently there are some things we don't need to know about people. In our church, if people want to work with the children, we do a background check on them. If they want to work in security, we do a background check. If they want to work around the finances, we do a background check.

Still, with all of the information resources available, there are things about people that can never be learned. There is no written record of it, and only they and God knows about it. This doesn't prohibit folks from speaking in tongues, dancing or clapping their hands with joy, but should serve as a reminder of the importance of consulting God in everything. No one has arrived yet. People are still very human.

As great as Paul was, he still had this limitation, this thorn in the flesh. Many have tried to label it, but they don't know, so I won't waste time telling what others have said. All I know is that the Bible called it a thorn, and thorns are sharp and sticky. When there are thorns around, individuals have to watch where they walk.

This is interesting. The week might be going wonderfully and suddenly thorn. God could be using a person and people will say that he or she blessed them, that God sent him or her their way, and still this person could have this serious problem. It's to remind him or her that he or she needs the Lord. The power is not in people; it's in Him.

The most important point was that God wanted to guard Paul against being puffed up. Pride is a real danger to all. It is one of the worst enemies.

I am told that most folks who get involved in sales do so because of the acclaim it affords them. They enjoy being in the spotlight. They love to receive certificates and awards because of the recognition it brings them personally. That said, I have found that most Christians also come to Christ because He acknowledges their worth. Before they knew Him, they were nobodies, and He offered them water that never runs dry. He offered to make them a new person. So they signed up. God has not promised huge mansions and enormous bank accounts down here, but He surely has promised a mansion in Glory.

> *In my Father's house are many mansions: if it were not so, I would have told you. I go to prepare a place for you. And if I go and prepare a place for you, I will come again, and receive you unto myself; that where I am, there ye may be also.*
> JOHN 14:2-3

God is not like man that He would try to fool people. If He didn't have it, He wouldn't have said He did.

He has planned the most wonderful time of recognition that anyone could ever imagine. Paul wrote of the soul winner's crown, the servant's crown and others, that God is preparing them for His people. There's nothing wrong with recognition, and individuals will get their share in eternity. It's all recorded in the book.

Aside from wanting to keep Paul from being puffed up, God wanted to reveal His power to this servant. The weaker the vessel, the more God is glorified when His power is revealed through that vessel. So, when Paul prayed three times for his thorn in the flesh to be removed, God said no. "My grace is sufficient to thee," He insisted. His love, His favor and His blessings are sufficient to help any and every believer walk through any type of suffering or weakness.

This word sufficient means "the power or strength to withstand any danger." God's grace within the believer can carry him through anything.

So what was God saying when He said, "My grace is sufficient for thee"? He was saying, "It's sufficient — if it is used." It's not that the grace isn't there. It's not that there's any lack or deficiency in God's grace.

There's an overabundance of grace available — if believers would just use it. I used to work in a pharmaceutical company, and every now and then they moved us around to the packaging area. Bottles would come down the conveyor belt filled with liquids or powders, lotions, potions or whatever. As a jar would come down the belt, it would turn on a laser beam, and that beam would activate a mechanism to place the proper label on the jar. Every once in a while, a jar would miss the light switch and that would cause it to miss the label and miss being placed in the right box. That particular jar of product never made it to the marketplace.

What does that all have to do with God's blessings? People can be on God's blessing line in His plan and destiny, but if a person misses the light, which can cause him to miss the mark and go astray. When one misses the mark and that individual misses his place and his blessing, that individual will also lose his or her recognition.

Never was God's grace insufficient. It was never that it wasn't enough. It was always sufficient — if it was accepted. Let nothing cause you to miss His grace for your life.

Paul's thorn in the flesh seems to have been either some sort of physical suffering or some sort of spiritual attack. Either way, it doesn't matter because God's grace is sufficient to see His people through whatever comes their way.

Every year, there is what many call "the flu season". During several months of the year, many flu cases are reported. The strange thing is that not everyone gets the flu at the same time. Some get it in winter. Others get it in spring time and some don't get sick at all. Then, every few years, an especially terrible strain hits. But God's grace is made perfect in weakness. The weaker the believer the more God can demonstrate His strength. It wasn't Paul's strength that was to be seen; it was God's strength. And His strength is "made perfect in weakness."

When God speaks here of weakness, He is not referring to someone who is continually falling. This weakness speaks more of inability. In a person's inability, God's ability is demonstrated. If people could stand on their own, they wouldn't need God. I don't seek my own remedies for the thorns that afflict my life. I look to God. I say, "God, You said that your grace is sufficient for all my weakness. I need You now." And that's when He holds me.

Paul went on:

Most gladly therefore will I rather glory in my infirmities that the power of Christ may rest upon me. Infirmities speak of weaknesses. I may be strong in some things, but there's another side of me that is weak. That's why God put Pastor Mamie in my life. She makes up for what I am lacking.

In the beginning, Adam seemed to be doing fine. Then God put him to sleep, took his rib out and made him an Eve. Part of Adam became Eve, and they then needed each other. Does that mean that all single people need to get married as quickly as possible? Not at all. Before God took that rib, Adam was whole. He didn't need anyone else. But when God decided that it was time for him to be married, He took a part of him and put it into someone else. So singles if you're not enjoying your singleness, you're living beneath your privilege of being a whole person.

Paul was not bragging on Himself, how good he could sing, preach and teach. He was bragging on the Lord. He knew he couldn't make it by himself.

He wanted the power of Christ to be demonstrated, clearly seen, in his life. This word rest means "to fix upon." The idea is that the power of Christ rests upon the suffering, just as the Shekinah glory dwelt in the Holy Place in the Tabernacle. In other words, God needs a place in His creation where He can rest. He is looking for some weak vessels that He can rest in. And when He rests in His people, He gives us grace.

God is looking for somebody through whom He can show off. He can't use those who think they have it all. He's looking for those who will say, "God, without you I'm nothing, but with you I can do all things."

The third point is that God wanted to teach Paul to live for Christ's sake. When Paul suffered from an infirmity or weakness, it gave Christ a chance to infuse power into him to overcome his weakness. If you have a problem with your attitude and the least little thing someone does ticks you off, that's where you need Jesus. Christ comes in where believers often don't think they need him.

Several years ago I warned our congregation that they should pray after every successful day. What did I mean by a successful day? I meant a day in which God used an individual mightily in some way to bless other people. That's when the enemy will hit a person. He wants to pump people up with pride.

Jesus is our example. He was either in prayer, coming from prayer or going to prayer. The enemy cannot keep God from using you, so he tries to cause you to be exalted because of it. That's the only way he can stop people.

Satan knows a lot about pride. It was pride that caused his own downfall from the regions of glory and splendor. He is enraged when he sees anyone worshiping God and being used by Him. All believers need to remain prayerful and sober.

Paul learned to take pleasure in his infirmities. Most people just want to get rid of the thing, and he did too. But when he learned that it was for his good, he learned to appreciate it. If the Lord has left a thorn in a person's life, He knows why it's there and when it's safe to remove it. Trust Him. Let Him finish His perfect work in you.

The power of Christ working in a believer can overcome any weakness or temptation. God's grace is sufficient for reproach, ridicule, insults, slander, rumor or whatever anything else. It is sufficient for necessities, hardships, needs, deprivation, hunger, thirst, lack of shelter or clothing or any other necessity. It is sufficient for persecution, verbal or physical attack, abuse or injury. It is sufficient in distresses, in perplexities, in disturbances, in anxious moments, in inescapable problems and in any other difficulties. Hear God saying to you today, "My grace is sufficient." Lift your head up and walk with it high, for God is on your side.

Not only so but we glory in what?

> *Tribulations also knowing that tribulations worketh patience and patience, experience. And experience, hope. And hope maketh not ashamed because the love of God is shed abroad in our hearts by the holy ghost which is given unto us for when we were yet without strength in due time Christ died for the ungodly.*
> ROMANS 5:3-6

This passage helps to understand the why of many of the things people are called on to suffer. Many Christians have forgotten what Jesus said about life in this world:

> *In the world ye shall have tribulation: but be of good cheer; I have overcome the world.*
> JOHN 16:33

I love that "but." Believers will have tribulation, but ... Because Jesus has overcome the world, Christians too can overcome.

> *Wherein we greatly rejoice thou for now for a season if need be ye are in heaviness through manifold temptation but that the trial of your faith being much more precious than of God that perishes though it be tried with fire might be found unto praise and honor and glory at the appearing of Jesus Christ.*
> 1 PETER 1:7

Have you ever watched that syndicated television program, Candid Camera? Jesus is saying to you, "Smile, you're on tribulation camera." He is urging you, "Take that test, and do well on it because I have overcome. Keep going, son. Keep praising your Lord. Keep dancing before Me." When people move forward by faith in Him, He smiles too.

Every time an individual prays saying, "Father, You said that You would not put any more on me than I could bear, so I'm just going to worship you," He smiles again. Christians can overcome through Him.

When people are treating you badly on your job because you are a believer, when the bank keeps turning you down for a loan and when ??, just keep praising God. Then one will have complete deliverance.

Sometimes people experience the heaviness of temptations. After all, it seems that God is a thousand miles away. But if we know that all trials are working for our good, it changes everything.

Paul wrote to the Romans:

> *The Spirit itself bears witness with our spirit that we are the children of God. And if children, then heirs. Heirs of God and joint heirs with Christ. If so be that we suffer with him that we may also be glorified together for I reckon that the suffering of this present time is not worthy to be compared with the glory which shall be revealed in us.*
> ROMANS 8:16- 18

When God allows people to go through some test or trial, He has in mind the end result, the reward, the spiritual growth, your promotion. When sickness comes, when family problems come, hold on to God. Victory is coming.

> *My brother count it all joy when you find yourself in divers temptations.*
> JAMES 1:2

Clearly this was written to believers. Believers will find themselves in diver's temptations, or tests. This should be expected in the Christian life. The only way to get promoted in school is to take a test. The only way to prove oneself capable for many jobs is to take a test. The only way to get into the armed services is to take a test. Tests are not bad things. They are necessary, and God uses them to see where folks stand with Him.

The next time your children are acting up, it may be just a test. The next time your spouse is acting up, it may be just a test. The next time you don't feel God's presence, it may just be a test. What should your reaction be to the tests of life? James declared that Christians should "count it all joy." Why? Because God is preparing to promote His people, and this one last test will determine if they are ready for promotion or not.

James went on to describe other benefits of trials and tests:

> *Knowing this that the trying of your faith worketh*
> *patience.*
> JAMES 1:3

When people get upset with people they have to deal with on a daily basis, they need some more patience. When people get upset with their children, they need more patience. When an individual gets upset with another, he or she needs more patience.

There is a reason why individuals go through the things they face today, and Christians can rejoice in God that He knows what He is doing. He is building patience. He is preparing His people for promotion. "Surely there must be an easier way to get promoted," some people think, but remember that God has the very best at heart when He allows the trials of life to assail believers. "Be of good cheer." The Lord Jesus has overcome the world and as His people you can too.

Chapter Thirteen

The Song of Deliverance

Then sang Moses and the children of Israel ... unto the Lord.

EXODUS 15:1

God knows how to put a song of deliverance within the hearts of His people. The deliverance needed by individuals may be very different from that experienced by the children of Israel, but our victory can be no less sweet. The Israelites sang a very specific song that spoke of Pharaoh's armies being drowned in the Red Sea, while God's people passed over safely to the other side. Christians no doubt have much to rejoice about, as well

The enemies that confront believers may not be called Pharaoh. They may have other names and other characteristics, but they are no less real. Just as the Lord assured Moses of final victory over his tormentors, He has promised believers "Complete Deliverance" over every enemy who dares to assail them.

The children of God have a right to sing. When God's mighty arm is revealed through freeing Christians from the enemy's torment of their bodies, minds and spirits, it evokes a song of praise to Him. No wonder the Israelites sang and rejoiced that day!

Some may not be capable of singing with the choir or of being called to sing a special musical number in a church service or crusade, but each can sing God's song of victory. For this is a song that is not unto men, but unto the Lord Himself.

Some individuals only sing in the shower, when no one else is listening. It sounds good to them — just as long as the water is running. But when the water stops, they stop too. They don't know the beautiful harmonies that make songs so enjoyable to listen to. But when your victory is in the soul, one cannot be silent. The song of deliverance must be sung unto the Lord.

This, of course, is the place of victory that Christians long to live in constantly, but how does one get there? How can the many enemies that lie in wait to to bring destruction? How should the many challenges life sends be handled?

The victory that came to Moses and his people and the deliverance they received began way back in the wilderness when God told Moses to use what was in his hand. He had something, some God-given power, some divine anointing, that would eventually cause his heart to sing in victory over the defeat of every enemy.

Years later, when David was confronted by the giant Goliath, he found that he had something in his hand, too–something that made him a giant killer and a leader among men. David was still just a lad, but the secret of his victory was in the power of God vested in him.

Many believers do not doubt the power of God. He can do anything. Nothing is too hard for Him. And there are times when He sovereignly reveals His hand in a given situation without any participation on the part of Christians. However, God much prefers to reveal His power through His people. He delights in making a young boy into a giant killer and in using a humble shepherd to defeat a great army like Pharaoh's. God desires believers to experience His supernatural ability. He places His power in the hands of His people and then He instructs them how to use that power to bring about the needed deliverance.

God's will for everyday life is much like the complete deliverance which the children of Israel experienced at the Red Sea. Christians were not destined to struggle through life, hanging on to salvation by their fingernails, striving to stay saved and be part of God's Kingdom. Christians were destined to be "more than conquerors" (*Romans* 8:37), to live in total victory, to rejoice in God's goodness, and to sing to Him songs of praise.

The enemy knows this well, but he is determined that it will not happen. For this reason, he attacks the bodies and minds of people. He attacks families too. He attacks businesses. He does everything he can to disrupt finances, health and happiness. He doesn't heed to God's warning:

> *Touch not mine anointed, and do my prophets no harm.*
> 1 CHRONICLES 16:22 AND PSALM 105:15

God could have prevented Satan from doing anything against His people, but He did not. Why is that? It's because God wants Christians to use the power He has given them to overcome Satan. When Satan tests the faith of believers, he affords them the opportunity to prove God's power in their lives. Will God's people stretch forth their hands and claim their blessings? Will they use what God has given them to obtain Complete Deliverance? Will they be able to sing the song of deliverance? Will they continue to live defeated and downtrodden lives? It's up to each individual.

In the Lord Jesus, each person has a wonderful complete assurance policy. Nothing can harm believers, but if that is true, why is Satan wreaking havoc in the lives of people daily?

Surely it is because either the benefits of our heavenly policy have not been realized, or the things necessary needed to bring that policy into effect have not been done.

Believers can see themselves reflected in the lives of the children of Israel. Their victory at the Red Sea is a reflection of God's perfect will for the daily lives of His people. The many wilderness struggles that followed them brought forth complete deliverance.

So people of God you can rejoice, because the day of your deliverance is at hand. Sing loud with a voice of triumph as you walk with the God of your deliverance. Live each day as a believer who is experiencing total victory and walking in **Complete Deliverance**!

To order additional copies of
Complete Deliverance
have your credit card ready and call
1 800-917-BOOK (2665)

or e-mail
orders@selahbooks.com

or order online at
www.selahbooks.com

Printed in the United States
36212LVS00003B/178-240